Investing Against the Tide

Investing Against the Tide

Lessons from a Life Running Money

Anthony Bolton

Prentice Hall
FINANCIAL TIMES

An imprint of Pearson Education
London ■ New York ■ San Francisco ■ Toronto ■ Sydney ■ Tokyo ■ Singapore
Hong Kong ■ Cape Town ■ Madrid ■ Paris ■ Milan ■ Munich ■ Amsterdam

PEARSON EDUCATION LIMITED

Edinburgh Gate
Harlow CM20 2JE
Tel: +44 (01)1279 623623
Fax: +44 (01)1279 431059
Website: www.pearsoned.co.uk

First published in Great Britain in 2009

ISBN: 978–0–273–72376–9

British Library Cataloguing-in-Publication Data
A catalogue record for this book is available from the British Library

Library of Congress Cataloging-in-Publication Data

Bolton, Anthony.
  Investing against the tide : lessons from a life running money /
Anthony Bolton.
        p. cm.
  Includes bibliographical references and index.
  ISBN 978-0-273-72376-9 (cased : alk. paper) 1. Investment advisors. 2. Portfolio
management. 3. Investment analysis. 4. Investments. I. Title.
  HG4621.B65 2090
  332.6—dc22

                                                                2009000633

10 9 8 7 6 5 4 3 2 1
13 12 11 10 09

Typeset in ITC Stone Serif 9/14pt by 3
Printed and bound in Great Britain by Henry Ling Ltd, Dorchester, Dorset

The publisher's policy is to use paper manufactured from sustainable forests.

Contents

Acknowledgements

'I would like to acknowledge the whole investment team at Fidelity who have been invaluable in the preparation of this book. Many have read drafts and given excellent suggestions as to where they felt the text was unclear and needed more explanation or where there were subjects that I hadn't included and should have done so.'

Letter about Mr Johnson – Fidelity's founder

Mr Johnson's perspective on investment stars

From: *Institutional Investor*, July 1984

Sir,

Your article on Jerry Tsai appearing just a few pages from Edward C. Johnson's obituary took me back twenty years, to the day Jerry handed in his Fidelity jersey. All the Fidelity wholesalers were in town for our annual session with the wizards, and Jerry's loss was heavy stuff. How could you fire up brokers in Oshkosh without the Jerry Tsai story?

Mr Johnson called us together and said something that not only proved prophetic but has been useful when other stars have dropped from other teams. 'Never forget,' he said, 'that stars give their best performances on their way up. This is true in sports, the arts and business. Once there, they seldom repeat.'

Then he continued with the most important part: 'And when they leave,' he said, 'it opens the way for another member of the team to step up and create his own legend.'

He concluded: 'So don't worry. We've designed the system to let talent develop, and the system is alive and well.'

That was vintage Mr Johnson. He knew how things worked.

Duvall Hecht, Boettcher & Co., Denver

Anthony Bolton's portfolio management assignments

FIF Special Situations Fund	Dec 1979 – Dec 2007
Fidelity Special Values plc	Nov 1994 – Dec 2007
Fidelity European Values plc	Nov 1991 – Dec 2001
FF European Growth Fund	Oct 1990 – Dec 2002
FIF European Fund	Nov 1985 – Dec 2002

Foreword

One of the privileges of writing a foreword to any book is the opportunity to shape a reader's impressions by offering what may be called the 'first word'. So I am delighted to tell you that the book you hold in your hands contains the insights of one of the best investors on earth.

To succeed in investment you have to work at it. Watch for the importance of hard work as you turn these pages. Note how often going the extra mile on research and analysis is what accounts for sustained success. Keep your eye on that theme and you'll see that what the media call investment 'genius' actually springs from a base of sustained, unending research – which, in turn, yields a decisive information edge. That edge, plus steady nerves, flexibility, good judgement and a complete lack of bias or pre-judgement is what has enabled Anthony Bolton to deliver record-setting compound returns for decades. In this book Anthony describes in detail how he looks at investment and the methods he has employed so successfully over the years.

I stress hard work, an information edge and flexibility because few clichés have done more damage to investors' wealth than the phrase 'play the market'. Far too many people think stock-picking in particular is a game, or a gamble, like roulette, with luck playing a central role. Yet stocks are not lottery tickets or gaming chips. They are unique, ever-changing shares in specific companies run by real people, operating in fluid markets and economies against distinct, ever-changing competitors.

There is always a reason why individual stocks soar or slump. And that information can be found, often enough, in plain sight. But that doesn't mean finding it is easy. Every stock has many, many dimensions, objective and subjective, to consider. And the conviction needed to buy – or sell – should build up to the decision point from many, many discrete elements of fact and analysis. So while chance does play a role – undeniably – a wise investor would be well-advised to heed of the words of a great American sports manager, Branch Rickey: 'Luck is the residue of design.'

Even in today's information-rich environment, in which any investor can access data once reserved for senior Wall Street analysts, ferreting out which of the thousands of publicly traded companies have the best chances of growing, raising their earnings and thereby lifting their share values remains a demanding discipline. Perhaps even tougher is deciding when and why to admit – and let go of – the inevitable mistakes. We all make them, numerous ones every year.

What distinguishes investment winners, as you'll see in this book, is the willingness to dig deeper, search more widely and keep an open mind to all ideas – including the idea that you might have made a bad call. He or she who turns over the most rocks, looks over the most investment ideas, and is unsentimental about past choices is most likely to succeed. *Investing Against the Tide* shows us these concepts being stress-tested by one man's unique experience. It gives us a glimpse into the mindset and methodology of a truly remarkable, world-class investor.

What we find is a man whose convictions grow from immense research, a knowledge base that gives him the strength to hang in through sometimes prolonged contrary market trends. Yet he never yields to ego-driven stubbornness. The same disciplines that shape a decision to buy continue to apply to current holdings. Neither prejudice nor nostalgia clouds his decision to sell when a stock's fundamentals deteriorate. Living through that process vicariously makes this book something more than just interesting for readers. It is a useful experience, a live tutorial they can study, enjoy and even be changed by as investors.

Speaking of 'luck' as the residue of design, Fidelity is indeed fortunate that one of our savviest senior leaders, Bill Byrnes, spotted the high talent in Anthony Bolton well over a quarter-century ago. Since 1979, he has been an increasingly vital franchise player for Fidelity International. That is not only because his funds have delivered such spectacular results, and drawn so many assets, but also through the influence of his work-style and his judgement on a generation-plus of Fidelity analysts and portfolio managers.

That influence has continued in 2008 as Anthony dialled back from daily, full-time fund management to becoming a trusted mentor. There are few people I have ever met more suited for this new role. For all his world-beating accomplishments, Anthony is a model of geniality and of collegiality. Not surprisingly, for someone seeking an information edge, he is a great listener. And he is an open-handed sharer of ideas. Conversation with him is 99 per cent light and maybe 1 per cent heat, because he is 'cool' in the very best, most 'British' sense of the word – passionately unflappable, intensely calm. These are capital qualities in a money manager. And his depth and breadth of knowledge is unsurpassed – as you, dear reader, are about to discover. I certainly have.

Of the dozens of stocks Anthony and I have discussed over the years, one that springs to mind is Body Shop International, a company that we both owned at various stages of its evolution. I recall many talks over the best part of a decade about how that initially promising firm went awry, spent years in the financial doghouse, and then emerged with a stronger balance sheet, much-improved operations and what proved a winning strategy

– right up through its takeover by L'Oréal. I'd like to thank Anthony for our lively exchanges of views on the changing fundamentals of this company – among many others.

Let me close this 'first word' with the observation that commentators have graciously drawn a comparison between my own investing style and Anthony Bolton's. Over my own years as a fund manager, I have received a fair amount of coverage and comment, most of it actually quite generous. But being linked with Anthony Bolton is one of the greatest compliments yet. It puts me in the very best of company.

Peter Lynch

'I do not know what I may appear to the world but to myself I seem to have been only like a boy playing on the seashore and diverting myself in now and then finding a smoother pebble or a prettier shell than ordinary, whilst the great ocean of truth lay all undiscovered before me.'

Sir Isaac Newton

Disclaimer

Introduction

I began writing this introduction at 36,000 ft on a Boeing 777 on my way to the Caribbean. It's December 29 and the markets have almost closed for 2007; only Monday December 31 remains and I am one day away from giving up the Fidelity Special Situations Fund, the fund I have run, day in, day out for twenty-eight years. This marks my retirement from active fund management and stock-picking. It's a strange feeling – an activity that has occupied some point of my every waking day for those twenty-eight years and the two to three years before this that I ran money. Although I am resolved that this is what I want to do creating more time for my other interests, there is a bit of me that's sad. That said, I will not miss the daily mounds of information that a fund manager these days has to absorb – the reports, the emails, the voicemails, the meetings, the interactions with a team of more than thirty managers and sixty analysts. I can't quite believe I won't have to read another company's preliminary statement, examine a balance sheet, take notes of what another chief executive tells us, discuss the best ideas of an analyst or send another trade to my trader. In fact, I'm sure I'll still be doing some of these things in the future. However, one thing that I really want to do is to try and pass on the essence of what I've learnt over the past thirty years or so, first to my colleagues – and this will be my most important activity over the coming year or so – but also to a wider audience, hence this book. A lot of the material here is based on discussions that I've had with my investment colleagues at Fidelity and I have already used much of the book's contents to help train our analysts and new fund managers. Although the first book that Jonathan Davies and I wrote contained some explanation of my investment approach, my aim here is to expand on what I've learnt in much more detail. This book is aimed at both professional investors and the more sophisticated amateur investor, although I hope much of it will be of interest to most private investors.

There is very little that's new in investment and I will refer to important things I have learnt from other investors and quote widely from them (and I hope I'll be forgiven if I say something here someone else has already said and not given them credit). The quotes I have chosen are ones that I have found particularly useful in running money. What is original is the way I have blended all the ingredients together. As the accomplished investor Nils Taube (who sadly died while I was writing this book) once said, plagiarism is the key to good investing – and I fully agree with him. Investing is such a beguiling activity – it appears so easy at first; but if you talk to most professional investors they will admit to finding it harder than they thought it would be. Also, I have seen many bright, hard working and dedicated individuals that would normally succeed at whatever they put their hand to fail at investment. Why? It is much more difficult than it appears, particularly to do well consistently. Buy low/sell high is not easy.

❝ Buy low/sell high is not easy ❞   I have called this book *Investing Against the Tide* to reflect my contrarian approach to investment, being happy, and often more comfortable, swimming against the prevailing flow. It is organised into two main sections. The first is called 'Principles and practices from a life running money'. In this part I look at what makes a good company; how we go about company meetings; how I evaluate managements; how I look at shares; the importance of sentiment; and how to put shares together in portfolios. I go on to discuss company financials, balance sheet risk and my biggest mistakes, valuation techniques, mergers and acquisitions, recovery stocks, trading and how to use technical analysis. I then look at information sources, using brokers, market timing and macro factors, some observations on fund manager performance and which twelve attributes, in my view, make a good fund manager. In part 2, called 'Experiences and reflections from a life running money', I discuss some of my more interesting meetings, my best and worst investments as well as how the business has changed during my time in it. I end with some final observations on the investment business.

At the beginning of the book is a letter about Mr Johnson's (Fidelity's founder) views on investment stars, which I believe sums up some of the unique qualities of Fidelity as an organisation. I also list my portfolio assignments.

Although, as I say, I hope I have written the book in a way that an experienced amateur investor will derive something from it, I'm afraid at times the jargon may let me down, even though I have tried to avoid this and to give explanations wherever possible. On the other hand, this is not meant to be a textbook in the sense that it will contain detailed definitions of terms such as cash flow or enterprise value, so I assume knowledge of these.

Later in the book I go into much more detail about what makes a good investor; although the longer I've been in the business the longer I particularly value two attributes – common sense and temperament. If you can think logically, objectively and independently and 'keep your head when others are losing theirs', you have the starting blocks to being a successful investor.

Anthony Bolton

One

Principles and practices from a life running money

How to assess a company and the role of meetings

'Mean reversion is one of the great truisms of capitalism'

'Many shall be restored that now are fallen and many shall fall that are now in honour'

Horace (quoted at the start of *Security Analysis* by Ben Graham and Dave Dodd)

'You should invest in a business that even a fool can run, because someday a fool will'

Warren Buffett

What to look for in a business

I always start when looking at a share by assessing the company I'm investing in. How good a business is it? How sustainable is its franchise? Businesses are not created equal – some are much better than others and most businesses vary over time due to factors such as new competition or changes in the environment. Charlie Munger, Warren Buffett's business partner in Berkshire Hathaway, wants to understand a company's competitive advantage in every aspect – markets, trademarks, products, employees, distribution channels, positions relative to changes in society, etc. He refers to a company's competitive advantage as its 'moat', a virtual physical barrier that protects against incursions. Superior companies have deep, enduring 'moats'. He also considers the 'competitive destruction' forces that, over the long term, lay siege to most companies.

In general, it's easier to make money owning businesses with strong franchises than ones with weak franchises. The ability of a company to survive is important. Often, I ask myself a very simple question: 'How likely is this business to be around in ten years' time and to be more valuable than today?' It's surprising how many businesses fail this test. It may have a business model that meets market factors and demands today, but it is near impossible to predict that this demand will still be there ten

> **❝Superior companies have deep, enduring moats❞**

years from now. Another important question to ask is, how much does a particular business stand on its own two feet: how does it exist relatively independent of the macro factors around it. For example, businesses that are very sensitive to interest rates or currencies are less good businesses than ones that are insulated from such factors. An exporter of commodity products would fall into this sensitive category. A few years ago, I remember only too well looking at a medium-sized, UK-based chemical company that exported most of its product to the continent. At the sterling-euro exchange rate at the time it had a good business but I worked out that, if the currency moved 15 per cent against it, it might have no business or at the very least a substantially less profitable one. It wasn't difficult to decide to give that particular investment a miss. I like businesses that are in control of their own destiny and are not very sensitive to macro factors like this (though all businesses depend somewhat on the macro environment).

I also prefer reasonably simple businesses. If the business model is very difficult to understand I'm happy to pass on it – there are lots of others that are easier to understand. Sometimes it is possible to summarise the financial characteristics of a company in a few ratios. For example, when looking at banks the relationship between the price to book value and the return on equity is very important. Recently, a competitor argued that life insurance companies were often poor businesses because the ratio of overheads to funds under management could be too high (at say 2 per cent) to create long-term value unless high risks were taken on investments. Therefore, a single key financial ratio was at the heart of deciding the attractiveness of the business model.

> ❝ If the business model is very difficult to understand I'm happy to pass on it ❞

A really important characteristic I look for is whether the business generates cash over the medium term. I am convinced that cash-generating businesses are superior to ones that consume cash and this factor has generally given me a bias towards service businesses and against manufacturing in the portfolios I've run. Businesses that can grow without requiring a lot of capital are particularly attractive. Cash-on-cash return is the ultimate measure of attractiveness in terms of valuation. In playing off cash generation against growth, I generally prefer cash – as do most private equity investors. Very few businesses give compound returns above 10 per cent for any sustained period of time. Remember, mean reversion is one of the great truisms of capitalism. For most companies, the financial statistics used to evaluate their performance, such as sales growth, margins or return on capital, revert to the mean over time. This also applies to valuations and, sometimes, even management's ability!

> **ͶͶ A really important characteristic I look for is whether the business generates cash over the medium term 〃**

Meet the company

One of the main inputs for my investment process has been talking to the management of businesses either I'm invested in or looking to invest in. At an initial meeting with a company I've not seen before, most of the time will be taken up asking questions that allow me to build up an informed view of the business franchise – its strengths and weaknesses. The first meeting doesn't have to be with the chief executive; a good investor relations person at a company can be very helpful in describing the business in detail and helping me assess the business franchise. Of course, subsequently I will want to meet the executives as well.

Such meetings have changed greatly over the past thirty years. It used to be difficult to get to meet the management at many companies, particularly in Europe, and they often had a misguided view as to why we wanted to see them the first place. In the early days, if you got a meeting it would have to be at the company's office irrespective of where that might be. If it was in London, it was probably a group session (most often lunch at a broker's office.) Today they are, more often as not, individual, one-to-one meetings at our offices, although we still do a lot of visits to their offices and face-to-face meetings at conferences. An important service many brokers offer their institutional clients today is arranging such meetings – a glorified concierge service. A cynical broker acquaintance of mine observed that companies were in the visitor attraction business, a bit like a funfair, but for institutional investors rather than individual visitors. They are trying to make being an investor in their shares more attractive than another company's shares, hoping this both attracts potential investors and also keeps their shareholders on board for longer. This does have a ring of truth to it.

Preparing for a company meeting

Before I meet a company there are things I want to look at. First, I will examine a chart, probably the three, five and ten-year graphs to see how the stock has been performing. Then I will want to look at some valuation measures. I like to have as long a history as possible of valuation measures such as P/E (price/earnings ratio) price to book, price or EV (enterprise value) to sales and EV to EBITDA (earnings before interest, tax, depreciation and amortisation) – twenty-year charts if possible but, if not, at least a complete business cycle. Less than ten-year data I find can be misleading as they will not contain enough variety of business conditions. I want to be able to see how today's valuation compares with its history – is it high or around average or low against its history (of course, it's the low ones that really interest me). Then I will look at a chart showing the history of director deals. I will look at a list of the top twenty shareholders (the shareholder list is often wrongly ignored by investors, in my view). I'm examining whether it's diverse or concentrated, say with just a few investors controlling the company. Sometimes the names of the institutional shareholders will carry information because there are some I rate more highly than others and if one or two I rate are on the list that's a positive. I will also see how much of the company is held by insiders. I will look at a financial strength report (H-Score report, see Chapter 7), a chart showing the net short position and how it has moved over time, a chart of the credit default spreads where these exist, as it can be an early indicator of problems ahead, an indication of whether the company is liked or not liked by brokers and an indication of whether it's highly owned or lowly owned by the institutional investors. I will also look at a chart of earnings upgrades or downgrades so I can see at a glance whether average expectations are improving or deteriorating. Then I will want to look at the latest company results and any official releases (I am keen to be fully up-to-date with recent announcements so I can have a more fruitful discussion with management) as well as some press reports. Regarding results statements, I always like to read them in the original because managements spend a lot of time on the language and phrasing, which is often lost in a broker or press synopsis. I will then look at a few recent broker notes, if possible both positive and negative ones, and our internal analyst's notes and financial models. Finally, and most importantly, I will review my handwritten notes of previous meetings.

Although I like reading company reports in the original, I am more sceptical about company guidance. When companies give detailed guidance and say that their profits will be up or down by a specific amount, analysts write this down religiously. I will want to know how they get there and see if I agree with the assumptions on which that ultimate figure is based.

Meeting companies

Company meetings in our offices are normally with the chief executive or finance director of a company. The meeting is run by our analyst who follows the particular company and the analyst distributes a copy of his or her questions plus the latest financial models before the meeting. The meetings normally last an hour to an hour and a half (although occasionally I've done much longer ones and a few shorter ones). Very importantly, we like to set the agenda (with the exception sometimes of an initial meeting with a company or if they've come to see us to talk about a specific deal). We like to discuss the financial trends in the business as well as strategy, recent performance and new developments. Our discussion of trends can go into great detail about volumes, prices, gross margins, costs, operating margins, interest costs, taxes, etc., division by division. This helps us build up a more informed financial picture of the company. We would also discuss balance sheet items such as capital expenditure, working capital, debt and debt covenants. When we finish the meeting we really like to feel that we understand the business model and the primary factors that affect it; that we understand the strategy and have a fair impression of the management and their incentives; that we understand the business and recent trends – both areas doing well but also areas doing less well; their view of the outlook for the divisions of their business and the market generally, and finally that we fully understand the dynamics of the P&L, the cash-flow and the balance sheet, allowing us to build more sophisticated and accurate models than many of our competitors and most brokers.

❝ We like to set the agenda ❞

I will always try and spend the last few minutes (or the first few minutes, maybe while waiting for colleagues to assemble) to touch on a competitor, or a company they do business with, such as a supplier or customer. Although not all managements will talk about other companies, when they do it can be very revealing. The ultimate commendation is when a company talks positively about a competitor. I always put a strong weight on such a view. In fact, as a general rule, when a company says the opposite of what you expect them to say I put a double weight on it (for example, you normally expect companies to be sceptical of competitors). When they say what you might expect – like business is great across the board – I'm more sceptical and want, if possible, some form of independent confirmation. It is not that the majority lie, but there is a lot of 'spin'. Seeing through spin is one of the most important aspects of the job.

Finally, it is worth considering how risky the business model is – some businesses are considerably more risky than others. Often, this is because of the balance sheet structure, but sometimes this is down to the nature of the business. There is no better recent example of this than Northern Rock.

> **The ultimate commendation is when a company talks positively about a competitor**

There was nothing seriously wrong with the management or the business in general (although maybe the bank was too focused on growth). However, the business was much more wholesale-funded than its competitors (relying on funding from other banks as opposed to their own depositors). In most conditions this works. However, if conditions change, as they did in 2007, and the availability of wholesale funding decreases and its costs increase, this can put the whole model at risk. This is what we witnessed only too dramatically in July 2007.

> **Seeing through spin is one of the most important aspects of the job**

What to look for in management

'My recommendation is to invest in management you trust'

'When management with a reputation for brilliance tackles a business with a reputation for bad economics, it is the reputation of the business that remains intact'

Warren Buffett

'We also believe candour benefits us as managers. The CEO who misleads often in public eventually misleads himself in private'

Warren Buffett

'Getting to know the management of a company is like getting married. You never really know the girl until you live with her. Until you've lived with a management you don't really know them'

Phil Fisher

Get to know the management

Over the years I have come to value management integrity and openness more and more highly. In my early years of managing money I might have bought shares in a company where I liked the franchise but maybe had some doubts about the management competence or integrity. But not any longer. In the late 1980s and early 1990s I learnt my lesson with these types of companies the hard way. Despite the protection offered by outside directors and independent accountants, if a management really wants to mislead investors it has plenty of scope to do so and can get away with it for many years. Even if the management appears very competent, if they are not open then this is a significant disadvantage.

When I meet the management of a company the things I am trying to assess are their competence, their personal characteristics (e.g., are they optimists or pessimists by nature), are they more strategic or operational, how the management team works and most importantly how they are rewarded and what their incentives are. I often find that management who in a first meeting seem very impressive on subsequent meetings seem to regularly under-deliver so I really like those who give us a balanced view of their company and are good at delivering, or even better, constantly over-delivering, against plan. I find management competence can be best assessed by regular meetings with managers over an extended period of time and this is where we are very fortunate to have this kind of access. I find it more difficult to make an accurate assessment of management after just one meeting. When you meet the managers day in, day out, for many years you start to develop an antenna as to who might have the right qualities and who does not. Nowadays, if I have significant questions about a management team I will normally pass – there are always lots of other companies that make the grade on this measure.

It is very difficult to summarise what makes a good manager and how to assess this in a meeting, but the managements that normally impress me are those that have a detailed knowledge of the business – strategically, operationally and financially. They tend to be fanatical about the business, working long hours and demanding high performance and excellence from their team and they are reasonably self-assured and on top of what they do without being arrogant.

> **" The managements that normally impress me are those that have a detailed knowledge of the business – strategically, operationally and financially "**

Generally, I like companies where managers have a decent amount of 'skin in the game' in term of shareholdings (I prefer shares to share options, which are much more of a one-way bet). Also I want to establish that the objectives of management and shareholders are aligned. Sometimes, when I meet a large company where senior managers own only a few shares, I have the impression that their main incentive is the prestige and status (not to mention the perks) of running a large company and shareholder returns are lower on the list, despite what they may say.

In recent years I have become more interested in how managers answer questions and their body language as well as their reactions to certain questions. There are often questions that they are more uncomfortable in answering (not that we try to antagonise management – just the reverse, we hope meetings at Fidelity are something they enjoy more than their meetings with other institutions or hedge funds). Also, I may ask a question in the negative, so, for example, if discussing a UK company's manufacturing operation in China, instead of asking 'So, China's going well for you?' to which the reply might just be 'Yes', I would say: 'We hear some companies have found manufacturing in China more challenging that they first thought.' This should get a more interesting and emphatic answer.

One of the more important inputs into my investment process is watching share-dealing by insiders. Not that I would act solely on this measure, but it may confirm what other indicators are telling me. It can be a very useful lead indicator to a business improving or deteriorating. Every day I get a list of insider deals in UK companies that ranks the deals by significance. I would consider the size of the deals; whether it is a one-off or there have been several deals including other insiders; does the individual have a track record of buying or selling shares opportunistically; is it the chief executive or finance director (I will put greater weight on these than, say, a divisional director or non-executive). Some director share-dealing services argue that purchases are much more significant than sales. I would only partially agree with this. I would expect the founders of companies with big shareholders to reduce these gradually over time if the shares have done well, so I would put less emphasis on these types of sales (although the timing can carry information.)

Some of the most significant deals are when an insider does a different deal from what I was expecting. For example, the director who buys in size after the shares have already risen considerably or the director who sells after they have fallen a lot. Although not

❝ Watch share-dealing by insiders ❞ common, watch out for such deals because they can convey a lot of information. Even though today directors often give an explanation of why they did something, I put a lower weight on this unless I know the exact personal circumstances involved.

Another thing I've learnt is that people don't change. The tenure of the average fund manager is only a few years and because of this entrepreneurs who disappointed a decade or two previously sometimes return: many fund managers are unaware of or ignore their previous record. I generally avoid these situations, or if I do invest, I will have a foot closer to the door than I normally would. Someone who has let down or disappointed investors once is more likely to do so again.

My recommendation is to invest in management you trust. Warren Buffett said that he liked to employ or invest in managers he would be happy to see married to his daughter. I don't think you need to go that far but the sentiment it makes sense!

3

Shares – developing an investment thesis

'Every stock you own should have an investment thesis'

'You should look at stocks as small pieces of business'

Warren Buffett

'A stock doesn't know that you own it'

Warren Buffet

'Stock price movements actually begin to reflect new developments before it is generally recognised that they have taken place'

Arthur Zeikel

My colleague Peter Lynch said that you should be able to summarise in a few sentences why you own a particular company's shares in a way that even your teenage son or daughter would understand. This is excellent advice. This is your investment thesis and I would go on to say that you should retest this thesis at regular intervals. Although your investment thesis sets out the reasons why the stock is a good one to own, you should also think about what might lead it to become a bad stock (the counter thesis). It's a good discipline even if you own a share and know it's attractions also to be able to list negative factors about the share that 'bears' might latch on to. There will normally be some reasons certain investors don't like the shares regardless of how positive the outlook for a company and you should know why you disagree with each of the negative factors. In particular, I like to read broker research that disagrees with our views and then discuss with our analyst why they think the broker is wrong. Every stock you own should have an investment thesis.

At all costs avoid buying shares on impulses or tips. Peter Lynch used to observe that he found it strange that, say, doctors would buy oil exploration companies based on tips from friends, newspapers or brokers rather than use their medical knowledge to invest in biotech companies where they should have a better chance of being able to check out what is really going on. Invest where you have a competitive advantage.

> **You should be able to summarise in a few sentences why you own a particular company's shares in a way that even your teenage son or daughter would understand**

Warren Buffett's advice, to think of a stock as a small piece of business, is excellent. A good place to start when you buy a share is to look at it as if you were buying the whole business at that price. That said, we don't buy whole businesses. We buy shares whose price moves up and down. The share price adds an extra dimension.

Most importantly, you should forget the price you paid for a share, otherwise it can become a psychological barrier if the share price subsequently falls. The investment thesis is the key; check it regularly. If this changes for the worse and the share is no longer a buy and probably therefore a sell, you should take action regardless of the price being below what you paid. Trying to make money back in a share where you have lost money to date just to prove your initial thesis was correct is very dangerous. As a general rule in investment, it's not good practice to try and make it back the way you lost it. Luckily, I have a poor memory for figures and therefore seldom remember the prices I've paid for shares (which often comes as a surprise to outsiders!). I was recently asked by a portfolio manager whether, if I had a share where the investment thesis proved wrong but the shares subsequently fell to a very cheap level, should I keep the shares? My view was if the investment thesis was broken they should be sold even if the valuation was attractive.

I've never been one for setting price targets for each share that I hold, but I do like to recheck my investment thesis at regular intervals and assess my level of conviction. I prefer thinking in levels of conviction rather than in price targets. I just don't think in terms of this being a 20 per cent potential gain stock while another is a 50 per cent gain stock. Also, specific price targets suggest a level of precision about the future which I just don't believe is normally possible; price bands may be more appropriate. In general, many investors take comfort from very precise forecasts for businesses,

❝ You should forget the price you paid for a share ❞

thinking that if the forecast is precise it is more likely to be accurate. This is a dangerous assumption and generally not true. Sometimes when brokers give very specific targets I believe that they are attempting to suggest their ability to forecast is better than their competitors', which may not be the case.

❝ I've never been one for setting price targets ❞

In the short term, stock prices tend to balance buyers and sellers at a price that is just above the level most buyers are prepared to pay, but just below where sellers appear.

This is a fragile equilibrium. Small changes in the environment can change the balance.

In the long term, most share prices do follow the company's earnings, although over periods of one or two years the share price can become detached from earnings. Predicting earnings is therefore one of the most important activities of investment professionals and City analysts spend a huge amount of their time doing this, although assessing the quality of the business franchise is even more important in my view.

When I look at a share there are broadly six factors that I want to consider, all of which I go into more detail in other chapters of this book. The factors are:

■ the quality of the business franchise (Chapter 1);
■ the management (Chapter 2);
■ the financials (Chapter 6);
■ the valuation (Chapter 8);
■ the prospects for M&A (Chapter 9);
■ and the technicals (Chapter 12).

Sentiment – an extra dimension

'Successful investment is a blend of standing your own ground and listening to the market'

'One of your partners, named Mr Market, is very obliging indeed. Every day he tells you what he thinks your interest is worth and, furthermore, offers to buy you out or to sell you an additional interest on that basis. Sometimes his idea of value appears plausible and justified by business developments and prospects as you know them. Often, on the other hand, Mr Market lets his enthusiasm or his fears run away with him, and the value he proposes to you seems to you little short of silly'

Ben Graham

'[My] central principle of investment is to go contrary to the general opinion, on the grounds that if everyone agreed about its merit, the investment is inevitably too dear and therefore unattractive'

John Maynard Keynes

In the long run, the stock market is about the real valuations of business, but in the short run it is more about what people are prepared to pay for businesses. This can be quite different from their real value. To quote further, Keynes said in regard to the stock market that picking shares was like a beauty contest where 'it is more important to choose not who you think is the prettiest girl, but who the judges think is the prettiest'. Also, borrowing a phrase from Ben Graham 'the stock market is more of a voting machine that a weighing machine, at least in the short term'. Never forget this. The longer I've been in the business the more I've come to rate perception as being as important as reality. From a stock market point of view, we are most likely to be wrong when we all agree with one another on something. Perception is so important because when it builds to extremes it can overwhelm the intrinsic merits of a share for long periods of time.

I spend a lot of time analysing what sectors and companies are under-owned and unloved by investors and stockbrokers and

> ❝ The longer I've been in the business the more I've come to rate perception as being as important as reality ❞

which sectors and companies are over-owned. Generally, the risks of owning shares are much lower in the first category and higher in the second, or over-owned group. Again, as with many other factors I look at, I won't buy on this data alone, but it is one of the most important inputs into my buying and selling decisions.

Another feature of the stock market is that it's very difficult to insulate ourselves from the price action of individual shares – everyone's partially susceptible to this. Let me explain: the last few years I have been on holiday regularly to Forte dei Marmi, in Tuscany. If you go to the beach you will be approached by people selling clothes, food, jewellery, bags and watches. If you are interested in a particular item you need to bargain. My normal approach is to let the vendor mention a price and then offer a quarter of this price. However, it would be interesting if they let me quote the first price on the basis of what I thought would be a good price to pay. If I said I'd pay €50 for a bag I would be upset if the vendor accepted my first price outright. There would always be feeling that I had offered too much. The stock market has similar characteristics. For example, when a share sells at 100p and you work out that 70p is a good price at which to buy, if the price subsequently moves down to 70p you will begin to doubt your own calculations. Subconsciously, you start to think that maybe the seller knows something that you don't. The price itself influences behaviour – falling prices create uncertainty and concern, rising prices create confidence and conviction. Understanding this is a really important part of investing. All stock brokers know it's gen-

** Prices do carry information but don't be over-influenced by them**

erally easier to sell you a share that's in an uptrend and popular than one that's in a downtrend and unpopular. Because of human nature, a good investor must keep on trying to make himself or herself resist this tendency. As Warren Buffett puts it 'the key is that the stock market basically just sets prices, so it exists to serve you, not instruct you'. Prices do carry information (otherwise technical analysis would be of little use) but don't be over-influenced by them.

Behavioural science makes useful observations about typical investor behaviour. These are some of them:

■ We need to keep an open mind. Once we buy shares we become less open to the idea that our decision to buy was wrong. We close our mind to evidence that doesn't confirm our initial thesis.

■ We need to think independently of others. You are neither right nor wrong because the crowd disagrees with you.

■ Many supposed experts are not. Many experts never change their view. They remain with a permanently positive or negative view of the world or companies knowing they will be right part of the time. A number of stock market newsletters, surprisingly, get a high number of readers despite taking this approach.

■ We all think we are better at investment than we are. We are all overconfident and, in particular, you mustn't let a good run go to your head.

■ We are often most influenced by the recent past and by recent prices. Often the first plausible answer is the one that influences us.

■ We are too conservative when we take gains and too relaxed in running losses.

■ We should ask ourselves if we own it, would we buy it again at this price?

■ Investors underestimate the likelihood of rare events happening when they haven't happened recently, while they overestimate them when they have. A classic example of this is the effect hurricanes have on the insurance business. After a bad season investors often think the next season will be bad again. This point about investors being particularly influenced by their recent experiences is a very important one.

Successful investment is a blend of standing your own ground and listening to the market. You won't be successful if you are too much in one camp and ignoring the other.

How to construct a portfolio of shares

'A portfolio should reflect a 'start from scratch' portfolio'

'The great personal fortunes in the country weren't built on a portfolio of fifty companies. They were built by someone who identified one wonderful business. With each investment you make, you should have the courage and the conviction to place at least 10 per cent of your net worth in that stock'

Warren Buffett

'Sell a stock only when you have found a new stock that is a 50 per cent better bargain than the one that you hold'

John Templeton

'When an investor focuses on short-term investments, he or she is observing the variability of the portfolio, not the returns – in short, being fooled by randomness'

Nassim Nicholas Taleb

Although picking stocks is at the heart of building a portfolio, how stocks are combined to make up a portfolio is also very important. Even though Warren Buffett would argue that most portfolios are too diverse and good investment ideas are not abundant, most professional investment managers will own at least forty to fifty shares. In my case, the amount of money I ran grew considerably over the years and as a result I had no choice but to run a more diversified portfolio than this. I did this to maintain my traditional significant exposure to medium and smaller companies. Many observers think wrongly that I had chosen to have a lot of holdings. This was not the case. My ideal portfolio would contain about fifty holdings.

I have never run portfolios with much regard to the composition of the index. I am aware where my overweight and underweight positions are, but generally I do not try to decrease my underweights where I don't have conviction. I generally don't want to own shares unless I believe them to be valuation anomalies. I won't hold a share just because it's a big part of the index unless I have positive conviction. Also, I don't spend too much time on performance attribution. I strongly believe that too much performance analysis leads to a portfolio manager spending too much time looking in the rear-view mirror and correcting yesterday's mistakes by doing what has been working rather than identifying what will work in the future. Most investors want to do today what they should have been doing yesterday. If you just had a poor week or month or quarter, some portfolio managers think by studying past attribution it will somehow help them manufacture good performance for the next period. Sadly, investment doesn't work like that; you can't say I've done poorly but now I'm going to try harder and definitely do better. There is little short-term linkage between effort and performance. You should, of course, learn from past mistakes but it doesn't guarantee anything about the future.

> **❝ I have never run portfolios with much regard to the composition of the index ❞**

The three questions I ask are:

- does my portfolio match my conviction levels as much as possible;
- am I aware of the risks I'm taking;
- finally, is there anything to learn from my mistakes (there nearly always is something.)

A portfolio should, as nearly as possible, reflect a 'start from scratch' portfolio – i.e. if you were putting together a new portfolio from cash, what would be your holdings and weights in each stock? One of the things that I do each month is an exercise that helps me measure my conviction. On a piece of paper I write five headings across the top: 'strong buy', 'buy', 'hold', 'reduce' and '?'. I then write down every stock I own in the fund under one of these five headings. As well as helping me formalise my conviction, it highlights stocks where I need to do more work, such as reviewing in detail the pluses and minuses, getting more information from our analysts or asking for another meeting with management if we haven't seen the company for some time. Quantification of your conviction level is a very important part of successful investment.

Warren Buffett said: 'Charlie and I would much rather earn a lumpy 15 per cent pa over time than a smooth 12 per cent. After all, our earnings swing widely on a daily

❝ Don't spend too much time on performance attribution ❞

and weekly basis – why should we demand that smoothness accompanying each orbit that the earth makes around the sun.' This summarises my approach to investment. I always aimed for the highest average returns that I could from the portfolio over the longer term, even if it involved a more volatile performance record over individual years. I know this is less in keeping with some modern risk measurement methods. In terms of portfolio risk, as well as knowing the shape of your portfolio in terms of sector and stock bets, you should also be aware of any unintended bets in the portfolio (like having a high exposure to companies that are exposed to currency weakness). However, I would argue that most of the risk in a portfolio lies at the stock level and that's where I concentrate most of my risk control.

Investment management is all about making mistakes – a 'hit' rate of 55–60 per cent is good. All you need to outperform is a few winners and to avoid the losers – try to win by not losing too often. Remember that, on average, at least two in five of your investment decisions will be wrong. Probably one of these will be due to something changing after you have bought the shares and one because the thesis was wrong in the first place.

❝ Investment management is all about making mistakes ❞

The size of my bet in individual stocks normally reflects my conviction level for the stock, how risky it is, how marketable these shares are and the percentage of the equity I and Fidelity own. We put an absolute limit of 15 per cent on the maximum exposure as a percentage of the equity we will normally own in any company. I will then tend to alter the size of my bet as my conviction level changes over time, maybe increasing after a company meeting or a piece of company news or decreasing after a rise in the share price or a deterioration in the balance sheet. Since I've run large portfolios my policy has been normally to start with a 25 basis points holding in a company (0.25 per cent of the portfolio). As my conviction increases and subject to the constraints mentioned above, I would increase the holding going to 50 basis points (if I ran smaller portfolios I would start at 50), then 100, then 200 and finally 400. Occasionally I may go above 400 in a mega-cap share, but most of the time the company would need to be a FTSE 100 company for me to go over 200 basis points. With my holdings in many companies I am moving in a certain direction until something happens that leads me to reverse direction. Importantly, I don't normally make large adjustments to the size of my holdings in one go, my moves are more incremental. So while my conviction is growing I am in the building-up stage and when a share price appears to be more correctly priced I normally start to reduce my holding. Investment is rarely black or white.

I am often asked about my sell discipline. First, I try to avoid any emotional attachment to my holdings. There are three main reasons why I will sell a share: if something negates the investment thesis; if it meets my valuation target; or if I find something better. I often find that a good way to test my conviction in a stock is to find a similar company that I like and compare the two stocks directly. Normally, in comparing the two companies one on one, it becomes clear which I prefer after considering all the relevant factors. There can be a tendency for a fund manager, particularly in a bull market, to buy lots of holdings as they find too many things that they like. The direct way of comparing stocks one to one is a good way to whittle down the list. A bear market or consolidation phase is an especially good time to revisit your investment thesis on each holding and prune out those where you have less conviction. I normally reduce my number of holdings in bear markets.

I have always kept a 'watch list' of companies that I think are possible candidates to buy, but I don't yet have quite enough conviction to act on. One way I do this is to keep reports (both internal and external) and packs from company meetings on companies that are in this category in piles arranged alphabetically on shelves in my room. Normally, once a quarter, I review them to decide if I still want to keep them on this watch list. Some of my colleagues have seen me doing this sifting, going through the piles of reports and research on possible buy candidates, and wonder why I don't get my assistant to do all this. They don't realise that the process of revisiting these stocks helps me decide my conviction level. When I do my review I will divide the stocks into three categories: those I want to look at in more depth before starting a holding; those I'll keep on the watch list for another quarter; and those I'll remove from the list (of course, I can always return to review a stock during the quarter).

> ❝ A bear market or consolidation phase is an especially good time to revisit your investment thesis ❞

I keep my own files on any company that I own with all recent internal analyst reports, external reports that are important and accounts. There are also photocopies of my handwritten notes from company meetings. I will always refer to these files before a company meeting.

A portfolio manager needs to keep a good balance between 'offensive' investments and 'defensive' investments – 'offensive' is looking at new potential investments and 'defensive' is keeping on top of your existing holdings. With a small number of stocks in the portfolio this is not difficult however, when running a large portfolio with many holdings (I have had portfolios with up

ff A portfolio manager needs to keep a good balance between 'offensive' investments and 'defensive' investments **jj**

to 200 holdings), the tendency is to spend too much time on 'defensive' investment at the expense of 'offensive'. One of the things I do to make sure I don't fall into this trap is to use our in-house team of analysts to help me with the 'defensive' investments so I can devote most of my time for looking for ideas. This is one of the advantages of having a big in-house research team.

Assessing the financials

'If in doubt about how a company is doing, follow the cash'

'Cash is a fact, profit is an opinion'

Alfred Rappaport

A t Fidelity, we pride ourselves on our financial models of companies that we follow. All our analysts make forecasts covering two or three years for each company they research of the profit and loss account, the cash flow statement and the balance sheet. Each analyst will put a good amount of time and effort into their models of companies they cover. When portfolio managers and analysts discuss stocks, part of the discussion will involve the model (a stock is hardly ever discussed in detail without a model being referred to) and the portfolio manager will often cross-examine the analyst about their assumptions and the details of the models.

One of the most important outputs of the models are our earnings estimates. These compared with what we call 'smart street', i.e. the best amongst the broker analysts on a particular company. The difference between our forecasts and 'smart street' is an important input into our investment process. For some of my colleagues this is the most important input and they would rarely purchase shares where our estimates are below 'smart street'. To me, this is an important input, but I use it in conjunction with many other inputs. Occasionally, I will buy shares where our estimates are below street, particularly if the valuation is attractive enough and I know that I need time to build a holding. Spreadsheets make the preparation of models far easier today than they used to be, although the key to a spreadsheet is the assumptions behind it. This is where the real thinking is done.

When I joined the City, I knew very little about accounting and I don't think I ever properly looked at a company's accounts.

> **❝The key to a spreadsheet is the assumptions behind it❞**

Although over the years I've had no formal training, I've taught myself to read accounts and become reasonably proficient at analysing them. Being able to read accounts is a requirement of the job. I've discussed elsewhere the attractiveness of free cash flow and this is one of the attributes I will look for in a company I'm examining. If in doubt about how a company is doing, follow the cash. Also, I put a lot of weight on the balance sheet. Another thing I've learnt from experience is to read the notes to the accounts very carefully. Vital information about a company can be hidden in these notes (where the company sometimes hopes it may be overlooked).

Although I always like reading the management's original statements, I put particular weight on what is said in a market listing or share issue document. Every statement the company makes in these documents has to be independently verified (unlike the company's usual statements) so the company has much less latitude to use spin or make statements where there is little evidence to back them up. These documents can therefore be particularly useful, especially if they are not too much out of date, so, when looking at a new company I find these documents a good place to start. As investment opportunities, initial public offerings (IPOs) are often less attractive in that the seller sets the timing and the pricing. This is particularly the case with offerings from private equity sellers when they are selling all their holding or a major part of it, even though the seller should leave some margin for the buyer.

Once, company presentations were normally only available to institutional investors in private meetings. Today, these, as well as all a company's announcements and accounts, are normally available on its website, making such data available to anyone. I strongly recommend looking at this information in its original form rather than relying on a second-hand summary such as a broker's note. The web has substantially increased the information available to investors and I recommend making full use of it.

chapter

7

Evaluating risk

'Highly geared companies are particularly exposed if business conditions change for the worse'

'Never invest in a company without understanding its finances. The biggest losses in stocks come from companies with poor balance sheets'

Peter Lynch

'Even in such a time of madness as the late twenties, a great many men on Wall Street remained quite sane. But they also remained very quiet. The sense of responsibility in the financial community for the community as a whole is not small. It is nearly nil. Perhaps this is inherent. In a community where the primary concern is making money, one of the necessary rules is to live and let live. To speak out against madness may be to ruin those who succumb to it. So the wise in Wall Street are nearly always silent. The foolish thus have the field to themselves'

John K. Galbraith

When I've analysed the biggest mistakes I've made over the years they have nearly always been in companies with poor balance sheets. When something goes wrong at a company with a weak balance sheet this is when equity investors lose the most. The job of the professional investor is as much about avoiding disasters as it is about picking winners. Most fund managers can select their share of winners, but what will often differentiate a good portfolio manager from an average one is holding fewer losers. Many fund managers just don't take balance sheet risk seriously enough. Even in my last year or so of running money, four of my worst performing stocks were Isoft, SMG, Erinaceous and Johnson Services Group. In each case, the company suffered from debt or liabilities that made the equity particularly exposed if the business started to deteriorate – and they did. By design, none of these was a big holding. Buying a highly geared business is not dissimilar to buying an ungeared business on margin. Often when things start to go wrong the bankers will force the company to make disposals of divisions, but the market will often spot they are a forced seller and the offers for the division will be reduced to levels below what the company and investors thought they were worth (one of the risks inherent in using sum of the parts valuations for highly geared companies).

❝ The job of the professional investor is as much about avoiding disasters as it is about picking winners ❞

For a long time I've used a service called Company Watch to help me keep on top of companies with weak balance sheets. Sometimes it's obvious that a company is poorly financed but sometimes its not. Company Watch calculates a H-Score, a twenty-first century version of the Z-Score, for each non-financial company it follows. To make it possible to predict problems in any company, it compares a large sample of the financial statements of businesses that got into financial difficulties in the past (the 'failed group') with those that did not. This enabled Company Watch to build mathematical models that can be applied to any company to determine the extent to which it reveals the characteristics of the failed group. Companies are scored on a financial health rating of 0 to 100 with 100 the strongest. Companies in the lower quartile have sufficient of the characteristics of failed companies to render them vulnerable. It is very unusual for companies with scores higher than 25 to experience financial distress. The models consist of seven key interactive measures, ratios that are treated mathematically and weighted before being combined to produce the single measure, the H-Score. In support of the H-Score, each of the seven measures is scored as well, to reveal and evaluate any company's financial strengths and weaknesses over the past five years. Scores are recalculated every time a company produces financial results.

The H-Score is one of the inputs I review every time I look at a company. Also, any company in my portfolio that is in the weakest quartile gets my special attention. A bit like technical analysis it's not that I say I'll never own a company with a poor chart or a poor H–Score but, if I do, I will want to do so with my eyes fully open and pay special attention to the company's progress. If something starts to go wrong, these are the holdings that should be sold early, even if this means selling the holding at a loss. Highly geared companies are particularly exposed if business conditions change for the worse. Generally, I will take a smaller holding in these types of company than I would if the balance sheet was stronger. The ones in the lowest decile or so are the most risky of all. Also, I watch very carefully companies that historically had good scores, but which subsequently enter the lowest quartile. I also look out for otherwise strong companies with a steadily declining H-Score and ones with a very volatile H-Score history.

I am always surprised how little analysis is done by most broker analysts on balance sheets. Sometimes I will read a report on a company that I know has a weak balance sheet and no reference will be made to this at all. When looking at liabilities you should look at both bank debt and bonds outstanding (although it is normally bank debt that gets a company into trouble) as well as being aware of other liabilities such as future payment obligations, pension fund liabilities and redeemable preference shares. You should understand the debt profile (particularly how much is repayable in under a year) and the covenants relating to the debt. Some companies have debt levels that vary a lot seasonally or during the month or quarter. In these cases, just looking at absolute debt levels at the half year or year-end may give a false impression that the company is in a stronger position than it actually is. It is also worth looking at the net interest figure as well as the debt figure. This can give an indication that average debt levels are higher (we will normally ask such companies in meetings what average debt levels are over the year as well as the seasonal pattern, not normally something companies publish). Finally, although most companies consume cash as they grow and release cash if they shrink, there are exceptions. For example, many contractors that have an element of customer advances actually consume cash if they shrink. You should be aware of these characteristics.

Company Watch sends me a list each fortnight of companies at risk (in the lowest quartile), companies that have entered the at-risk zone and companies no longer at risk. This is one of my essential pieces of regular reading. As a further check, in more highly geared businesses it's worth looking at where the debt trades (if it does trade). I've sometimes seen businesses where equity investors are quite cheery about the company when debt investors are paying a big discount on the debt. I would rather take my steer from the debt investors (if the debt is not worth near par, the equity may be worth very little.) It's also worth looking at credit default spreads where these exist for similar reasons.

Although buying companies with poor balance sheets has been my most common mistake two others factors I would highlight are:

- buying companies with poor business franchises;
- buying companies with poor management, management with suspect business practices or management who are not open with investors.

As a bull market progresses, portfolio managers have to beware of lowering their guard and buying lower quality businesses or management. As Ben Graham put it: 'Buying a low quality share when business conditions are favourable is risky.'

For the last 15 months of running my fund I was able to short individual shares through forward contracts as well as owning shares. In looking for shorts I normally wanted shares that had exactly the opposite characteristics of what I looked for on the long side (e.g. weak balance sheet, suspect management, poor business franchise, high valuation, high institutional ownership, loved by brokers, already performed really well and low likelihood of being taken over. Of course, normally you don't get all of these characteristics, but I would try and find stocks with a number of them). Thinking like a short specialist is a good discipline for most portfolio managers. I try to work out what are the factors that could unravel the story, where the businesses weaknesses are. If you are aware of what might go wrong in a company (knowing the counter investment thesis) one may be able to spot before others the fact that it is going wrong.

A useful test, to establish the downside in stock, is to assume that you are looking back from the end and the share price is half its current level. Can you create a believable scenario which gets you back to this price? If you can, beware – it may happen!

Finally, remember that bad news doesn't travel well (as the Galbraith quote at the start of this chapter explains). There are lots of factors in the system that try to contain poor news while the investment manager's job is to try and discover it. Some people will definitely know that something is wrong at a

❝ Thinking like a short specialist is a good discipline for most portfolio managers ❞

company, but they won't broadcast this fact. Only by diligently talking to a number of informed sources, normally off the record, will you be able to unearth these situations. It can take time and effort to put together the pieces of the puzzle. For example, in the Nick Leeson Barings Bank scandal, the counterparties to the deals knew that something untoward was going on, but they had every incentive to keep that information to themselves. No doubt some people knew of problems at Bear Stearns before their announcement.

❝ Remember that bad news doesn't travel well ❞

Or course, most companies use debt and debt is not normally bad news. Companies that use debt sensibly can increase returns substantially for equity investors. Others have inefficient balance sheets today, and here shareholders should be asking for more debt. If I had my time again in running my funds and had avoided every share with a bottom quartile sector H-Score I might have missed a few winners, but I believe I would have avoided most of my disasters.

How to look at valuations

'One of the few compasses we have are historical valuations'

My whole approach to investment is to buy shares that represent what I believe to be a valuation anomaly in the stock market and then wait for the anomaly to be corrected. Hardly ever would I buy a share where I believed the valuation appeared correct. Now, it is easier to spot an anomaly than knowing exactly when it's going to correct and therefore I like to have time on my side. So normally I buy on a one- to two-year timeframe with, over the years, a fairly consistent average holding period of eighteen months. However, I am very happy to be patient and, if I still believe that my thesis is correct, I will wait several years if I have to. I'm often told by our analysts: 'Yes Anthony, this share is cheap, but I don't see a short-term catalyst'. I tell them that in my experience it's very unusual to see a significant anomaly and at the same time the catalyst that will correct it (if it was that obvious the anomaly wouldn't be there in the first place.) By buying cheap shares (particularly with strong balance sheets) you have a margin of safety. By having a portfolio of anomalies, although I find some are in the 'gestation' phase, I do normally find I have several that are working and starting to be revalued. Since I've been running large portfolios it normally pays to be early so I can accumulate a big enough holding while there are still sellers around; once a recovery becomes obvious such shares are more difficult to buy. I have found that valuation anomalies are more likely to be found with medium-sized and smaller companies and this is one of my reasons for focusing on them. However, from time to time this changes as has been the case over the past year or two with the many of the largest companies in the UK looking undervalued relative to the rest of the market.

One of the few compasses we have to navigate the choppy waters of investment are historical valuations. As I mentioned in an earlier chapter, I like to know the long-term valuation history of a particular stock or

> ❝ Buy shares that represent a valuation anomaly in the stock market and wait for the anomaly to be corrected ❞

sector, if possible twenty years or more but

"" By buying cheap shares you have a margin of safety ""

always containing at least one full business cycle. Knowing what range of valuations is normal for the type of company or for a particular industry is invaluable, particularly when valuations reach abnormally high or low levels. Of course, this is less useful if the business mix has changed significantly over time. Buying when valuations are low against history substantially increases your chance of making money; while buying when they are high increases your risk of loss. This approach has been at the heart of my approach to investment.

I'm often asked what my favourite valuation measure is. My answer is always that I don't have one, but that I like to look at a range of valuation measures. In fact, I believe it dangerous to dwell on only one measure. Most measures I will want to look at both on a relative basis and on an absolute basis. Although most of what we do is about

"" Buying when valuations are low against history substantially increases your chance of making money ""

making relative comparisons you should never forget absolute valuations, particularly at market extremes. For most companies, and particularly for non-financial ones, I look at five main types of ratio. My first is the old fashioned P/E. Normally I look at the ratio of the price to predicted earnings in the current year and up to the two following years. As well as the absolute PE I will look at the relative PE. Then I will look at a prospective ratio of the Enterprise Value (EV) to gross cash flow or EV/EBITDA making sure the EV is adjusted for items such as minorities and pension fund deficits. Then I consider the prospective free cash flow i.e. the prospective cash the company is expected to generate per share divided by the share price. I will look at the price to sales chart or even better, if it's available, an EV to sales chart (these measures are particularly useful for companies making losses or low profits). The fifth measure is a valuation method that looks at the cash flow return on investment (CFROI) in relation to how the share price trades relative to invested capital. Businesses that make returns above the risk free rate are expected to trade at a premium to their invested capital and vice versa.

The main sources I use for these types of valuation are CSFB Holt, Quest (owned by Collins Stewart) and the CROCI methodology used by Deutsche Bank. These types

> **❝Never forget absolute valuations❞**

of valuation tools have come into prominence only in the past ten to fifteen years. I use all three systems particularly for screening for possible buy ideas and for cross-checking against other valuation methods, although they do share some of the disadvantages of discounted cash flow valuations. Also, you need to learn which valuations are most appropriate to use for which industries. For example, price to adjusted book value is most helpful for housebuilding shares. PE ratios for these shares are pretty meaningless because of the once-off nature of profits on land sales. Despite this, I am always surprised that well known investors will quote PE ratios when describing the attractiveness of this sector.

Two valuation methods I have less time for are PEG (price to expected growth) ratios and dividend discount or discounted cashflow models. I realise that PEG ratios are more the domain of the growth rather than the value investor but I'm afraid I can see little logic in the argument that a business at five times earnings growing at 5 per cent a year, one at 10 times earnings growing at 10 per cent or one at 20 times earnings growing at 20 per cent, which all have the same PEG, as being equally attractive. I would go for the 5 times earnings growing at 5 per cent every day. Regarding discount models such as dividend discount or discounted cashflow, these make specific predictions of dividends or cashflow for ten consecutive years followed by a terminal value when the business is assumed to be in a mature state. These are then all discounted at a discount rate and added up to get today's value. The trouble with such valuations is that most of the value is from year four or five into the future and not the next few years. In my experience it is difficult enough to predict the next two or three years accurately enough let alone the period beyond that. Changes in the assumptions for the later years can substantially alter today's valuation so I would only use these types of valuations as a cross check, while being very aware of their shortcomings. I do not initially look at the yield, because over time dividends are affected by earnings and I prefer to look at earnings valuations. However, in protecting the downside, yields, where these are safe, are very useful. I will also look at other valuation tools such as break-up values. However, the investor should be aware that some valuation measures are more 'robust' than others. What I mean by this is that as a bull market progresses I find that the valuation tools used by brokers to justify valuations often becomes less and less conservative. Break-up values, particularly if they are not based on hard values such as cash or prime property, tend to gain in use as a bull market progresses. In a bear market the opposite happens with perhaps towards the end more conservative measures such as dividend yields being talked about much more than usual. Even if a company has no profits a clever broker will always find some other ratio that makes the shares look attractive! Be on your guard for these less conservative valuation methods.

> ❝ As a bull market progresses valuation tools becomes less and less conservative ❞

Takeover targets

'A bias towards medium and smaller companies will help your odds of holding companies that get taken out'

Oautne of the nice things about owning shares is that occasionally they get bought out at a premium. The average premium on a buy-out is 25–30 per cent above the last trading price and sometimes, particularly if there is competition, the bid premium can be considerably above this. I believe that by identifying shares that are more likely to be bid for, an investor can increase the odds of shares in their portfolio becoming targets.

It is rare for mega-cap stocks to be bid for and therefore a bias towards medium and smaller companies will help your odds of holding companies that get taken out. This may seem obvious but is often forgotten. There are normally two types of bidders for companies: industrial companies who are often (but not always) companies in a similar line of business and financial buyers such as private equity firms. In the former camp, you should be able to identify industries where consolidation is more likely. I remember when there were many regional listed TV companies in the UK. Today, most of these have been merged into ITV and this was a well flagged process. A similar trend has taken place in the tobacco industry with many national companies being merged into a few global ones. In some cases, monopoly rules will mean certain mergers are impossible and it is important to understand these dynamics and where national monopolies are less of a problem as, say, with tobacco.

> **One of the nice things about owning shares is that occasionally they get bought out at a premium**

Why mergers happen

Although bids from private equity are sometimes for industrial reasons, more often than not, it's the financial characteristics of a particular company that makes it attractive to private equity. All things being equal, bidders prefer companies with steady, predictable cashflow. This is because the new companies can take on significantly more leverage (debt) than the management was willing to take on while the business had outside shareholders. Because private equity buyers can gear up the company and most profits are then offset by interest, they don't generally pay much corporation tax and therefore valuations based on EV/EBITDA are particularly relevant. What they are prepared to pay will depend on the appetite of bankers for such deals and where bond markets are trading. The first few months of 2007 marked an exceptional time for private equity deals with banks prepared to lend money with few or no covenants (very unusual!). The £11 billion takeover by Kohlberg Kravis Roberts (KKR) of Alliance Boots probably marked the top of the cycle in terms of the high valuation paid and the size of the deal and I don't suppose we'll see another like that for a very long time. Most of the time the financial ratios that attract a private equity buyer are the same ratios that attract a value investor (also the things that put you off as an investor also deter private equity, such as pension fund liabilities that are large relative to the market capitalisation). Therefore a value approach should increase your chances of holding companies that might be bid for. Private equity is likely to remain a force in the markets and public to private deals will return, once the current indigestion is over, particularly as their funds have become larger and larger leaving fewer and fewer opportunities for them to purchase large companies outside public to private deals on the stock market. We have seen a number of smaller deals in 2008 and firms buy back at discount the debt in deals they made in 2007.

Another area I touched on in an earlier chapter and which can give a clue to the likelihood of a takeover is an analysis of the shareholder list. To start with, if a company has a controlling shareholder or group of shareholders, as many European companies do, a takeover will be at their discretion. However, companies with one or two large, but not controlling, shareholders can be more vulnerable, as are companies controlled by a handful of institutional shareholders. Such shareholders give the company's shares 'optionality'. A bidder will know that if they get the agreement of two or three of these large shareholders they are well on their way to success. Uncontrolled companies with lots of cash surplus to the business can be particularly vulnerable. Most bidders will want acceptances of over 90 per cent of shareholders even though anything over 50 per cent means they've succeeded. At 90 per cent they can compulsorily buy in the rest of the shares. Some private equity bidders will need to know they can do this because their financing structures rely on 100 per cent access to the target company's cash flow. As a result, a shareholder with 10 per cent is in quite a strong position in such bids and may, in some circumstances, be able to prevent a bid succeeding. There have been circumstances where Fidelity didn't have the full 10 per cent, but with one or two other shareholders we were at that level and we and these other shareholders have agreed not to accept a bid because we believed it too low.

In my experience, other institutions' staying power may not be as strong as our own and I've had several cases where initially they agree with us but as the bid enters its final period they change their mind, not wanting perhaps to end up owning an unlisted share. Where we have had a full 10 per cent plus ourselves we have had some success in not accepting a bid, staying in the subsequently unlisted company, and being bought out or seeing the company re-listed at a much higher level. However, it doesn't always work out favourably. One notable exception was a company called Sinclair Montrose, whose main business was providing temporary doctors and nurses to hospitals. We thought the offer from private equity was too low and kept our shares in the company even though the listing was withdrawn. A year or two later there was a major change in the business environment when their biggest customer, the NHS, set up in direct competition. This was a bad development and profits collapsed. Unlike a listed investment, we had no opportunity to get out of our investment, even at a loss.

A very profitable example of a successful bid company for us was MMO2, the mobile telephone company that started as a spin-off from BT. Shortly after the spin-off I asked the chief executive what he thought would happen to the business in the medium term and he said quite openly that he thought they would be bought by one of the big telephone companies. This happened a few years later when they were bought by Telefónica. It was this comment plus other attractive recovery characteristics of the shares that led me to make MMO2 for a long while one of the biggest holdings in my fund. At the time I always preferred it to Vodafone because the latter had little chance of being taken over.

Often acting on tips, many investors try and spot shares they think will be taken over in the short term. This, in my view, is a way generally only to create commission for the brokers. I am very sceptical of being able to predict M&A targets in the very short term and buying on tips is one of the surest ways to lose money. Once a bid has been announced, however, I find many investors are too quick to sell out. As the final price paid is often above the initial bid, it is best not to sell after the first bid announcement unless you identify risks that will prevent the bid being successful. Merger arbitrage professionals only focus on investing in these types of situations and I do believe with careful analysis they can be a good way to make money.

> **❝ I am very sceptical of being able to predict M&A targets in the very short term ❞**

In most of this chapter I have focused on target companies. What about listed companies that make the bid? Normally I find, if there is a strong reason for making the acquisition and a sensible price is paid, this can be very positive for the acquirer's shares over the medium term. I am, however, sceptical about the 'transformational' deal that is 'so rare that it can't be missed' and the acquiring company as a result pays a very high price to make the deal happen. When it comes to financing a deal most companies will use bank debt and/or bond markets. If it has to

resort to unusual financing structure, as, say, convertible preference shares, this is often a warning sign that conventional
channels were not open to them. Be sceptical of these types of
deals. At the height of the private equity bubble in the first part
of 2007 I went on record as saying that I was worried about
'covenant-lite' loans. From a private equity shareholder's point of
view, these loans, with little or no restrictions on the financial
performance of the company involved, were attractive (normally
loans have covenants attached where, if the financial performance of a company deteriorates to the extent that certain preset
ratios or covenants are breached, the loan can be recalled by the
lender). They were even used by a competitor investment management firm doing a management buy-out.

My favourite type of share

'The heart of my approach has been buying recovery or turnaround stocks on attractive valuations'

'We average down relentlessly. Two things seem pretty clear to me: first, no one can consistently buy at the low or sell at the high (except liars, as Bernard Baruch said), and second, lowest average cost wins. We constantly strive to lower the average cost of our positions by buying more if and when the price drops'

Bill Miller

At the heart of my approach, particularly in the Special Situations Fund, has been buying recovery or turnround stocks on attractive valuations. These are normally businesses that have been doing poorly, perhaps for some time. Many investors, in my experience, don't like to be associated with businesses that are not doing well and can miss when a change for the better occurs. This often involves changes in the management team, a restructuring or even a refinancing (or a combination of these). In a similar vein I like unpopular shares. Peter Lynch liked shares with one or more of the following characteristics: Does it sound dull, or even better, ridiculous? Does it do something dull? Does it do something disagreeable? Is it a spin-off? Is it disregarded and not owned by institutions or not followed by analysts? Do rumours abound involving something like waste or mafia ownership? Is there something depressing about it? Is it a no-growth industry? These are all characteristics that tend to put off the majority of institutional and private investors and can lead to attractive investment opportunities.

> **I like unpopular shares**

A great sign often comes when analysts give up on a company and there are few people making forecasts on the business. Another opportunity can arise in companies coming out of bankruptcy or Chapter 11. I've done well with these types of company such as the cable TV companies, Marconi and Eurotunnel. They tend to be completely off most equity institutional investor's radar screens. In a similar vein are companies with complex or unusual capital structures, which put off many investors.

The best recovery stocks in my experience are those where new management comes in who can demonstrate that the company in question lags behind its peers on a number of fronts and they have a clear plan, which normally involves doing lots of little things better, to return it to performing in line or better than its competitors. If these factors are measurable so much the better, because you can keep track of how the new team is doing and how far along the recovery path they are. Retailing, where it's often said 'retail is detail', is a good source of these types of recovery situations. You must not confuse a recovery situation in an underperforming but otherwise satisfactory business with a company with a poor business franchise; these may never recover.

How to buy recovery stocks

Often you need to buy a recovery stock before you have all the information and it doesn't feel comfortable making the purchase – don't be put off by this. By the time all the information is there and the recovery is established, an investor will have missed some of the most rewarding times to own the shares. Sometimes investors must force themselves into this 'discomfort' zone. However, on the downside it's very easy to be too early in recovery stocks and this is the mistake many investors make. I will sometimes take a very small holding at this stage (say 10 basis points) which helps me focus on the stock and then add as my conviction grows that the worst is over. It is an important observation that the first bad news (such as the first profit warning) is rarely the last. A warning sign of more bad news to come can be what are called 'brave face' trading statements from managements. They tend to be general and bland and not very specific about the future. So a recovery buyer must be patient, especially in timing his main entry point. Where you have conviction, averaging down is a good strategy, as Bill Miller points out. Since I've run large funds I have had to be early anyway and buy when there are shares available. Often our own analysts can finesse their ratings on shares and go positive just as the share price starts to recover. I've needed to be at least one move ahead of this, so I can have accumulated a decently sized position before it's clear that things are improving and when there are still sellers in the market. A particular situation that occasionally occurs is one where the shares of a particular company decline for some time in anticipation of an event for the company that is well known and perceived to be bad for the company (such as a big lawsuit or a new entrant into their market). Often, by the time the event arrives it is well in the price and buying just beforehand makes sense.

Another type of situation I like are companies with asymmetric pay-offs – stocks where you might make a lot of money but you can be confident you won't

> ❝ The first bad news (such as the first profit warning) is rarely the last ❞

lose a lot. An example of this would be an attractively valued oil exploration company with sustainable cash flow from existing wells and a strong balance sheet that reinvests this cash flow in exploration including some wildcat wells where the reward can be very high if successful. A company like Cairn Energy has done this very successfully, twice discovering 'company maker' fields. I am less keen on symmetric stocks, where one may do very well or do very badly, unless the odds are really attractive.

> ❝ I like companies with asymmetric pay-offs ❞

As well as recovery stocks I like companies selling at a big discount to their assets, unappreciated growth stocks (maybe in areas unfamiliar to many investors or maybe having a growth division that is hidden within a company whose main business is less attractive), valuation anomalies in a particular sector (say the cheapest stocks in a sector that I don't think should be the cheapest) and takeover targets. Of course, these criteria are not mutually exclusive.

Jeremy Grantham, chairman of GMO, makes some very interesting observations about growth and value investing in the US: 'Growth companies seem impressive as well as exciting. They seem so reasonable to own that they carry little career risk. Accordingly, they have underperformed for the last fifty years by about 1½ per cent a year. Value stocks, in contrast, belong to boring, struggling, or sub-average firms. Their continued poor performance seems, with hindsight, to have been predictable, and, therefore, when it happens, it carries serious career risk. To compensate for this career risk and lower fundamental quality, value stocks have outperformed by 1½ per cent a year.'

I couldn't put it better than this. I know where I want to place my bets given these long-term odds. Of course, over shorter time periods one particular style can outperform for several years before the pendulum swings back the other way.

How to trade

'The stock market gives you lots of "mulligans"'

I n my early days as a fund manager, when I ran a smaller and more concentrated portfolio, I used to do my own trading as well as picking the stocks in my portfolio. I believe it helps to have direct experience of buying and selling. However, it is very time consuming and it's a much better use of resources to have a dedicated trading team. The relationship between the portfolio manager and their trader is very important. A good trader will learn when a manager may want to pay up and when they won't. Also they will know what news is important to pass on and what is just part of the daily 'babble'.

In the past ten years I've become a keen fly fisherman – not that I'm very successful, but it's an enjoyable way to pass a few hours (and forget the stock market). I think there are some similarities between fishing and trading. When you have a fish on the line you have to know when to pull them in and when to give them more line. In the same way, knowing when to be aggressive in buying or selling and when to stand back and let the market come to you is part of the skill.

For a long time most of my orders have been bigger than the immediate size available in a particular share and therefore it normally takes me hours or days to buy or sell the position I want. For this reason, the availability of a block of shares if you are buying (or the bid for a block if selling) is very important. Nearly always the cheapest way of buying or selling in size is via a block if this is available. Therefore it's very important that our traders see all the block trade possibilities that are available and occasionally it's the actual bid or offer of a block that, in itself, will make me act (for example if it's a small company on my watch list). We also have a dedicated person sitting separately from our traders and behind a Chinese wall who helps handle sensitive blocks of shares for us. I particularly like to see internal blocks of shares from other Fidelity managers and this is the cheapest of all trades to execute. (One of the reasons this happens is because different funds can have very different cash flows in and out of the funds and we occasionally get one portfolio manager selling a share when another is buying it; also, different managers have different styles so, for example, a value fund might be selling when a growth fund is buying.)

" The cheapest way of buying or selling in size is via a block "

I only set limits on a minority of my trades and normally I give my trader full discretion. If the price moves more than about 3 per cent against me he will nearly always refer back to me any way. Where I do set limits I've always avoided round numbers. My argument is that most investors think in terms of round numbers and set limits at multiples of 10 or 100 – so if a stock is trading at 98p they will say buy up to 100p or if it at 93p they will say sell down to 90p. I always like to go just over or under the round number, so in this example my buy limit would be 101p and sell limit 89p. This can be particularly relevant in applying for placings or new issues, where again most of the crowding of orders is at round numbers. I believe that avoiding round numbers slightly alters the odds of being able to execute a particular trade in my favour.

Most of the money I've run has been in open-ended funds (funds where investors can add or redeem their investments daily, leading the fund to grow or shrink). I've

" I only set limits on a minority of my trades "

needed to have a reasonable amount of liquid holdings to meet potential redemptions, although with a large fund redemptions are typically not large in relation to the size of the fund. The market generally overprices liquidity and less liquid investments are more attractively priced, even though they are less easy to trade. This is another attraction of less liquid, smaller stocks.

Another thing I found is that it's rare that you only get one chance to make a trade at a specific level. Unless the news item is very significant and, if you are patient, you normally get a second opportunity once the initial excitement has died down. Bill Miller, chairman of Legg Mason Capital Management, likened this to the golfing term 'mulligan', which means a second shot you can take without penalty. The stock market gives you lots of 'mulligans'.

12

Technical analysis and the importance of charts

'Technical analysis forces you to cut losses and run profits'

'The truth is more important than the facts'

Frank Lloyd Wright

When I look at a stock almost the first thing I will want to review is the stock chart (normally a three or five-year chart) because I like to put today's price in the context of the stock's recent price history. I will look at a stock differently if I know it has performed really well over recent years compared with one that has been falling for a long time or one that has moved sideways. When I hear an interesting new story on a company that I haven't looked at for a while, one of the first things I will want to know is if am I early in hearing this or have many other investors already bought on the same attractive arguments: the stock chart will often tell me this at a glance. Where a stock has done very well, say tripling or quadrupling in value, then a lot of the good news must already be in the price. I am normally wary of these stocks. An example of this came in 2007 after four years of a bull market when many cyclical manufacturing and metal company shares were up three or four times (some more) from their 2003 lows. This was on the back of exceptional demand for their products or output from Asia and in particular China. I remember one of my younger fund manager colleagues, fresh back from a trip to China, saying to me that the China demand story was one of the most attractive he had heard for any group of companies that he had looked at. My observation was that it was indeed a very attractive story but how many other investors had been influenced by the same argument before him? The most successful investors had already bought these shares probably in 2004, 2005 and 2006 (I was too early in my caution, as the stock did very well until mid-2008; then they started to decline). This does not

> **The first thing I want to review is the stock chart**

&& I dislike 'pass the parcel' stocks &&

mean I will never buy a share that has already done very well (in fact, occasionally, this can be a great opportunity) but I will treat such shares as being substantially more risky particularly if I think a market turning point is near. Even 'great' fundamental stocks where investors have big unrealised profits are particularly vulnerable to setbacks. This is really important and not always understood by managers without experience. I particularly dislike what I call 'pass the parcel' stocks – those where the valuation is very high but they still have good momentum and investors hope there is a bit more to go and they can sell them to someone else before the music stops.

Why technical analysis?

My interests in technical analysis started with my first job at the small bank, Keyser Ullmann, in the early 1970s. I remember clearly that when I went for my interview fresh from university the investment director showed me a chart of the price of Marks and Spencer shares and then went on to draw investment conclusions from it which, I'm afraid, meant very little to me as I knew nothing about analysing charts in those days, although I nodded knowingly! Keyser Ullmann had three full-time analysts; an economist, a fundamental analyst and, unusually, also a technical analyst – a wonderful gentleman called Arthur Abrahams whose two main interests in life were charts and collecting Victorian paintings (he was early in spotting the merits of that wonderful painter Atkinson Grimshaw and he was always telling us what good investments the paintings would be and how right he was). Anyway, Arthur taught me a lot about charts, how to use moving averages and relative strength, how to interpret patterns that indicated break-ups (or break downs). I remember making one of my first investments, a tin mining company whose share price chart had made a significant break-out. I think I invested about £100 and made about £20 on it. This was also one of my very few share investments because when I started to run a fund I stopped buying individual shares personally and instead put my money into the funds I managed. I think this should be standard policy for all fund managers. Since giving up my fund management responsibilities I have kept my personal investments in the Special Situations and Global Special Situations Funds and the majority of my stock market assets remain in these two funds.

The way I look at technical analysis today is as a framework or overlay into which I put my fundamental bets on individual stocks. I see it as a discipline for my stock picking. What I mean by this is that, if the technical analysis confirms my fundamental views, I may take a bigger bet than I would do otherwise. However, if the technical analysis doesn't confirm my fundamental positive view, it makes me review my investment thesis on a company, for example checking that there aren't negative factors we have overlooked. If my conviction is very strong I will often ignore the technical view; at other times if it conflicts I will take a smaller bet or reduce my position.

I've found technical analysis to be particularly useful on larger stocks in the UK for the FTSE 350 and in particular for the FTSE 100. On smaller stocks it can often take a professional fund manager running a medium-sized or larger fund days or even weeks to buy a position and here using a chart I find less useful. The largest companies are often the most complex and also the most difficult to analyse and, with these, the chart can be more useful in indicating something that is being missed. Very importantly, the trend can go on longer than expected in a very large company and I will use the technical input as a way to help time my entry or exit, or when to double up or halve a position. I look at the technical situation as a summation of all the fundamental views available on a stock at that particular moment and it can sometimes be a warning signal of problems ahead. In a world where every professional fund manager knows that at least two out of five share picks they make will not work out as they hoped this is very useful.

I will also use charts as screening tools for highlighting stocks where I should look at the fundamentals of the company in more detail; an example would be recovery candidates where they can be helpful in indicating a change of trend.

It may sound surprising that, in my view, which system of technical analysis one uses is less important than the discipline of using charts in the first place. My advice is to try and find a system that works for you and then stick to it. I use two main sources as well as reading the output of several broker technical analysts. The first input is our internal technical team who are very useful: I sit down once a month formally with our chief technician to go through my holdings as well as going to their monthly review of world markets, which is open to all our fund managers and analysts. Also, we have an excellent Boston-based technician whose output I always read (Fidelity has always valued the information charts provided and has chart rooms in most of our offices).

❝ Find a system that works for you and then stick to it ❞

The main outside service I use is a US firm called QAS (Quantitative Analysis Service) run by a delightful gentleman called Mal Roesch who sadly passed away while I was writing this book. I first met Mal in the 1980s at a broker conference arranged by an Australian stockbroker in Wengen in Switzerland. I remember it well because on the first day we had company presentations all morning and then went skiing with the company executives and other fund manager delegates in the afternoon. The second day the presentations lasted to the mid-morning coffee break and then we skied. The third day, the agenda was supposed to have been the same as the second day, but at breakfast time the sun was shining and the snow beckoned. The organiser said: 'What the hell, let's forget today's presentations and head for the slopes.' I didn't learn much about the Australian companies we were meeting but I did meet Mal – and I've always been grateful for it.

Mal's system ranks most major stocks around the world (as well as market indices, currencies, commodities and interest rates) against the short and medium term and assigns them grades according to where he believes they are in their own price cycle. For example, a D7 or D8 is bottoming a stock; A1 and A2 are in up-trends; B3 and B4 are topping stocks; and C5 and C6 stocks are in downtrends. The inputs into the system are price performance of the particular stock over different time periods, both absolute and relative. I find it an easy system to use because, once you buy into his ratings, one can quickly review any market in the world and see what he likes and doesn't like (the stocks in a country are grouped by industry).

Almost every month since the meeting in Wengen, while I was running my fund, I had a call with Mal. He also visited our London offices two or three times a year. I describe my interaction with him as a bit like going for a check-up at the doctor – in that, as well as hopefully hearing good news; you may hear what you may not want to hear. On each call, as well as discussing the overall environment we went through the stocks I owned in the portfolio and Mal gave his views, whether positive or negative. Like anybody in the investment world, Mal was not always right, but on average he was more often right than wrong. When you're well known in investment circles, people won't necessarily always tell you what they really think, but only what they think you might want to hear (i.e. they tend to agree with your views). Mal was the exception, he was very happy to tell me one of my companies was 'ski-slope stock' (bad news!) or 'fall in love with girls not stocks' or more bluntly 'Anthony, it's a piece of shit'. It does every fund manager good to have their views cross-examined in this way from time to time.

> It does every fund manager good to have their views cross-examined

One of the great disciplines of technical analysis is that it forces you to cut losses and run profits – something that's always easier said than done. Although at heart I'm a fundamentalist I have definitely found that the combination of two approaches seems to work better than just one on its own. A few years ago I spoke at a technical analysis conference and said that if I was on a desert island and was only allowed one input for my investment decisions, it would be an up-to-date chart book. I think today I would still be of the same opinion. The trouble with fundamental data is that I can't single out only one source that on its own would be sufficient. I could, if pushed, run a portfolio with just a chart book – although on a desert island, it wouldn't be high up on my list of survival items.

A final observation on charts is that many financial statistics are best shown in charts. I like to view in a graphical form many of the ratios or factors on a company so I can see them in a historical context. Also, a chart is normally much quicker to read and this is very important when reviewing a wide range of data as I am, for example, before a company meeting.

Information sources I use

'In this business there is no shortage of answers – the skill is knowing whom to ask and what questions to ask'

'Probably the biggest intellectual problem an investor has to wrestle with is the constant barrage of noise and babble. Noise is extraneous, short-term information that is random and basically irrelevant to investment decision-making. Babble is the chatter and opinions of the well meaning, attractive talking heads who abound. The serious investor's monumental task is to distil this overwhelming mass of information and opinion into knowledge and then to extract investment meaning from it'

Barton Biggs

'In markets, everyone tends to see the same things, read the same newspapers and get the same data feeds. The only way to arrive at a different conclusion from everybody else is to organise the data in different ways or bring to the analytical process things that are not typically present...

As I have often remarked, if it's in the newspapers, it's in the price'

Bill Miller

In thirty years, the amount of information available to investors has increased enormously, as has the computing power available to process it. In the early days the job was very much about collecting data not available to others and a lot of the job involved the act of gathering this information. Today, it is much more difficult to find data others don't have; the job has altered from collecting data to analysing it. This is a very significant change.

I've always liked lots of inputs: lots of data, views, opinions and analysis. I seek views from a wide range of informed sources. I seek unconventional and different views and you never know where a good idea will come from. Therefore I like having lots of sources, and sifting and comparing them is at the heart of my approach. If I miss an investment opportunity in a share that has never been mentioned to me I am much more upset than at one I did look at but wrongly rejected. I always hope my net is wide enough that most good investment ideas will be fed into it by at least one participant. Ideas are pitched to me both by our internal analysts as well as all the outside brokers I'm in contact with. Here, I like to use some of the smaller specialist brokers as well as the larger investment houses, each having different strengths and weaknesses. I always consider my 'lifeblood' is the information provided to me each day by my internal analysts as well as the outside sources that provide information and views. This input comes in the written word, emails, voicemails, face-to-face meetings and telephone conversations. I like to try and go through this daily if possible, only feeling up to date once I have consumed my daily ration. The key is to know what you are interested in. A lot of what is sent to me I don't read more than the headline. Also, with most of my emails I get the headlines at least printed out as I find it easier to digest and sort quickly through the written word rather than text on a screen. If a piece of research seems just to confirm my view with no new interesting facts or features I won't read it. Most research nowadays is presented in a form that makes it easy and quick to digest the main points. There are normally two or three levels of summary before the main report itself. Over time, I've found some commentators more useful than others and I will spend more time on their output. I've spent years accumulating knowledge about who is useful and who is not.

> **❝ I like lots of inputs – you never know where a good idea will come from ❞**

In recent years I have become more and more interested in areas of research such as market research and experts whose views are not available to most investors. As research by brokers becomes more and more of a commodity product and more and more institutions hold one-to-one meetings with company management I have been very interested in increasing our competitive advantage through new sources. For risk of endangering this competitive advantage I can't here be too specific on some of our newer sources, but I think every good investment manager should ask themselves how they might independently check something and how they can develop sources of information not available to their competitors. In general, in this business, there is no shortage of answers – the skill is in knowing whom to ask and what questions to ask them.

The importance of brokers

'Never do business with people you have not met face to face'

People are often surprised to hear that, although we have a large internal research department, I still like a significant input from brokers. I use about forty – a list that includes most of the big, London-based investment banks but also some of the smaller more specialist, and in some cases regional brokers. I like to be able to put Fidelity analyst views in the context of the street and have a large number of sources feeding me ideas. Also, having an independent source of ideas means it's less likely that I will be trading at the same time as all the other Fidelity managers (which occasionally can restrict my ability to buy or sell in size).

However, there is a wide range of views at Fidelity about the added value from brokers and some of my colleagues don't use them much at all. They highlight that the broker's business model is not dependent on helping Fidelity make money for its clients. Also, hedge funds, which generally trade much more often than long-only managers, are moving higher and higher up a broker's client list and can get more favoured treatment as a result.

I find that the sales role is a very important one (the salesman is my main contact at a broker). They will filter the output of their firm, know my style and what it is that I'm looking for, but also have their own views and ideas (I am somewhat sceptical of the salesman that only passes on house views despite the fact that increasingly compliance officers at the broker might like this). They will also have a personal view of who they think are the best analysts in their firm and I usually like to meet these analysts. Broker analysts have an advantage (although occasionally it can be a disadvantage) that normally they cover a set of companies for much longer that the majority of our in-house analysts who change sector every two or three years. It's very important to realise that the written work at most brokers is censored these days (or the analysts know what they can't write). Therefore, calls and face-to-face meetings are very important to get 'colour' and find out what they can't put on paper.

Something else I ask my sales contacts to do is to highlight resources within their firms that are not widely used by the majority of their clients but that could be of interest to us. This could include meetings with their investment bankers or proprietary traders.

In terms of output I will normally see the majority of their written and quite a bit of their electronic output on UK companies, sectors, economics and strategy pieces, valuation screens, etc. When I ran European funds I used to see all their continental European research as well. I also get a few global strategy pieces and over the past three to four years reports on China and Chinese companies. I tell my salesmen that since 80 per cent of the research I get on companies are buy ideas I put extra emphasis on good sell ideas. Most of my sales contacts send me a mixture of emails and voicemails as well as writing handwritten notes on printed research drawing parts to my attention. I ask them not to duplicate messages on the same subject so either a voicemail or email is fine, but not both.

A colleague of mine in my early years at Fidelity said he would never do business with people he had not met face to face and I have followed his advice. As well as an initial meeting I like to sit down with my main broker contacts at least twice a year and I normally ask them to bring some ideas to that meeting. In an increasingly impersonal world I think knowing the person at the other end of the telephone and spending some time cultivating the relationship (even though you are the client) is important. Some investment managers believe, wrongly in my view, that the broker relationship is solely a one-way one.

In the past I have taken an interest in systems, such as Alpha Plus, which force brokers to be more specific on their recommendations and then measure quantitatively the success of these. Initially I thought this would be very helpful for me in deciding who was adding value and who not. Having used Alpha Plus for a while I am now more sceptical. I am a believer in broker capture systems such as the Marshall Wace TOPS system, which uses sophisticated computer software to manage portfolios solely based on broker salesman and analyst forecasts. However, I found Alpha Plus less useful the way I want to use brokers. The broker who came out best on Alpha Plus was not necessarily the one whose views I found most useful day to day. As a hedge fund manager I admire said to me one day: 'Anthony, you and I don't need the first call from a broker, we don't need to know the minute that they think a share is a buy or sell but we do need to know if they have a strong view and the reasons for it.' Initially I thought he was wrong but, on reflection, I realised that he was quite right.

15

Market timing and how the markets work

'A successful market timer must be able to go against the general mood of the market'

'You pay a very high price for a cheery consensus. It won't be the economy that will do in investors; it will be the investors themselves. Uncertainty is actually the friend of the buyer of long-term values'

Warren Buffett

'If we [the US in 2007] go into a recession we will come out of it. In any case we have had only two recessions in the past 25 years, and they totalled 17 months. As long-term investors, we position portfolios for the 95 per cent of the time the economy is growing, not the unforecastable 5 per cent when it is not'

Bill Miller

'Everyone has the brainpower to make money in stocks. Not everyone has the stomach. If you are susceptible to selling everything in a panic, you ought to avoid stocks and mutual funds altogether'

Peter Lynch

'The four most costly words in investment are: 'this time is different''

Sir John Templeton

Much of what can be applied to individual shares can also be applied to the market, although it's much more difficult to come up with a concept of fair value for the market than it is for an individual company. A bull market tends to climb the wall of worry, that is, at the bottom, all the problems are known and widely endorsed but gradually, as the market recovers, they lessen in investors' eyes. A good example of this has been the revaluation of tobacco shares in recent years. They used to sell on very low valuations despite their very defensive and predictable profit profiles; this was because investors worried about litigation threats and the fact that smoking was in decline in most developed economies. At the end of 2007 most of these issues had been forgotten (although it is fair

❝ A bull market tends to climb the wall of worry ❞

to say that the US litigation position has improved significantly). I am sure at some stage a bear market in these shares will develop again when investors remember that smoking can kill you. The environment for smoking in the western world and probably even in emerging markets is likely to deteriorate over the longer term. Always remember that bull markets paper over the 'cracks' while bear markets expose them – however, the point is that the 'cracks' are always there. It's a bit like one of those pictures that when you look at it one way you see a smiling face but if you look another way you see a grumpy face. The change is in how you look at the picture, not in the picture itself.

> **Remember that bull markets paper over the 'cracks' while bear markets expose them**

The stock market is an excellent discounter of the future – never underestimate this. It moves on what investors in aggregate expect to happen in the real world in six to twelve months' time. In my experience it's very difficult to predict the market's direction and particularly difficult to do so with any consistency. My advice (as given by many before me) is that investors should generally avoid market predictions and market timing. It is a common human tendency to become more optimistic as the market rises and pessimistic as the market falls because this is what the general news environment is doing. The most persuasive arguments about a rosy future are always most prevalent at the top and vice versa. Also, most of us have a leaning to be optimists or pessimists by nature and so are better at buying than selling if optimists (natural bulls) or selling than buying if of a pessimistic disposition (natural bears.) A successful market timer must be able to go against the general mood of the market and to some extent be able to control their own emotions. The more widely held the belief that a trend will continue, the less likely it is to do so. Professionals en masse have a very poor record in timing markets (but this is almost by definition because the majority can't be correct). Also markets tend to move eventually to make the majority wrong. Furthermore, over time, I believe that the conditions at market tops and bottoms have to become more extreme or unusual so that investors have difficulty identifying them. If spotting turning points was easy they wouldn't happen!

Given this, it's interesting that, the longer I have been in the business, the more prepared I have been to express my market views, although I am probably rather foolish to do so. However, I always preface my views by saying they are my personal views given with humility and I remind listeners and readers that I have only had really strong market views about half a dozen times in my career. Some general advice I would give to those attempting to time markets is that many bull trends go on for longer than expected. Also, after a strong sustained bull market, a new bear market can often have a few false starts before it really gets going (I think of it in terms of needing a few goes to kill the inbuilt momentum of the bull trend). Remember the long-term trend is up and so it's sensible to have an optimistic bias. If you miss a few of the good days in a bull market your returns will be considerably eroded.

> **" The stock market is an excellent discounter of the future "**

> **" The long-term trend is up and so it's sensible to have an optimistic bias "**

Bottoms and tops of the markets

Markets are more likely to make a V-shape at their lows (that is when a market has a final plunge down before a sharp recovery marks a new bull trend) than they are to make an upside-down V at their tops. Occasionally a market (but more often a stock or sector) will have a 'blow-off' top when prices move a lot in a day after a period when share prices have moved exponentially. This is usually a warning sign. At tops, it's not that the news stops being good, it's that it stops getting better, with the reverse at lows. However, it is extremely difficult to spot the catalysts that will turn the bull market into the bear and vice versa. An exception with bear markets is that the onset of a Middle East war has marked the market low in the two bears markets I've experienced. Here, markets had been falling for some time, most people knew a Middle East war or invasion was pretty likely and markets continued to fall until in one case, just after the war started, and in the other case, just before it started. This illustrates one of my more general observations on the market – when a very positive or negative event is widely expected for an individual stock or for the market overall, prices generally tend to make the most of their move in anticipation of the event rather than after it. However, more often than not, you won't see a catalyst like this. Sudden events do crystallise opinion, slow changes do not.

The general environment at market lows can be uncertain and worrying. I often say to my colleagues that it is normally darkest before the dawn just when you're looking into the abyss, feeling the financial system might collapse or no one will want to buy equities ever again and that's when the market turns, the bad news having, by then, fully permeated investment thinking and the last seller having sold. Markets bottom not because of the appearance of buyers, but when sellers stop selling and there is a similar process at tops. Watch investor cash positions closely. If these are high it is more likely that bad news has already been discounted. Don't expect companies to tell you when markets (or economies) are at a turning point; often they are less on top of trend changes than investment managers. A mistake that is made at market tops often happens after the first setback and a stock price reduction. Analysts will call the company in which they are investing, and will be told that business is great and that they haven't seen any weakness in demand for the product. This reinforces the 'buy' recommendation. However, the stock market is looking ahead six to twelve months; if the stock is up two or three times from the lows, a 10 per cent setback could still be very early days into the downtrend.

Always remember that the stock market goes in cycles and never goes up for ever. Sometimes when I've become more cautious after a long bull market others are doubtful, pointing out that the investment environment still looks very favourable. In my experience, after a long upward move is when you should be most on your guard, even if the outlook still appears very good. The question is not what is the outlook like, but what is being assumed in share prices?

> **" In my experience, after a long upward move is when you should be most on your guard "**

When evaluating the market outlook there are three things that I particularly focus on – and one that I don't consider. The one thing that I don't look at is the economic outlook, as this invariably looks great at tops and horrible at bottoms. In my experience, economic views won't help you time markets correctly. The three factors that I do look at are: the historical patterns of bull and bear markets, i.e., for how long and how far have we have risen in a bull market and how long and far have we have fallen in a bear market, when the length of time and the quantum of the rise or fall are high relative to history the odds of a change of trend increase significantly; I then look at indicators of investor sentiment and behaviour – indicators such as the put/call ratio, advisor sentiment, breadth, volatility, mutual fund cash positions and hedge fund gross and net exposure etc.. When these indicate extreme optimism or pessimism it normally pays to bet against them. Finally, I look at long term valuations, particularly ones like price to book or free cash flow. Again, when these move outside their normal range it represents risk or opportunity. When all three factors confirm each other, in my experience, the odds are that you are near a turning point. You won't spot the right day, week or month, but you should get the right quarter.

Despite having market views, I hardly ever made big market timing views in running my funds (the exception perhaps was

" Don't put money into the stock market you will need in the next three years "

managing the gearing in the Special Values Investment Trust). This is because I would rather bet on a number of individual stock views (knowing that I will get some wrong but that the probabilities should work in my favour) than have a major market view that, if I'm wrong, will reduce the whole portfolio's returns in a big way. I would describe my approach as more gradualist. My macro views have tended to set a direction for the portfolio and the type of stocks I am buying and selling. For example, if I believe we are in the mature stage of a bull market I will attempt to prune back my holdings of more risky stocks and those that have done particularly well. I will continue in this direction in a gradual way probably for some time until I believe the trend has changed and then I start to reverse this strategy.

When looking at macro factors and strategy, rather than start with my view of the world and derive a portfolio policy from it, I will tend to look at things the other way round; that is, I will look at consensus expectations for interest rates, inflation, stock and bond market returns and then ask myself where do my views differ from these consensus expectations and only bet where my views differ. This may be a subtle difference, but I believe an important one. Also, if I have a strong view that a certain scenario lies ahead I will test it by looking at what I expect the world to look like eventually under that scenario; then play it backwards to today and review whether it seems plausible. Working back from the end point often helps assess whether that view makes sense. Normally the sectors that have led one bull market are not the same sectors that lead the next one. For this reason I don't expect commodity and mining stocks to lead the next bull market.

Because hedge funds have grown in importance in the past decade or so, I believe that the average time length of a view, whether it be on markets or on individual stocks, has substantially shortened. I do think this has increased the opportunities for professional investors prepared to take the one to two year view rather than a time period measured in months or weeks. Often there is so much analysis of the branch or even the leaves on the branch, there are fewer people taking a view on the tree, let alone a view of the forest. This is an opportunity for those willing to take the wider perspective. However, my strong recommendation for private investors investing in shares is to take at least a three-year view if not a five-year view. Don't put money into the stock market you will need in the next three years (or if you do so be very aware of the risks that you are taking).

As Jeremy Grantham put it: 'The stock market fluctuates many times more than would be suggested by its future stream of earnings and dividends or by the GNP [gross national product], both of which are his-

> **❝ Never ever be wrong on your own ❞**

torically remarkably stable: i.e. the market is driven by greed, fear and career risk, not economics. Real risk is mainly career and business risk, which together shape our industry. Efforts to reduce career risk – "never ever be wrong on your own" – create herding, momentum and extrapolation which together are the main causes of mispricing.'

At the heart of stock markets are the two basic human emotions: fear and greed. On top of this are cyclical fashions that engulf investors over time. If you can stand aside from these elements, be aware of them and take advantage of them where relevant but never be engulfed by them, and be always aware of what they really are, you have the basics for being a successful investor.

> **❝ At the heart of stock markets are the two basic human emotions: fear and greed ❞**

chapter

16

What to do when you are not doing well

'The pressure –
when it's not
going well – is
intense'

'Most investors want to do today what they should have done yesterday'

Laurence H. Summers

've always thought that the best environment in which a fund manager could perform well was one in which they didn't know how they were doing. Unfortunately, the real world is the opposite from this and every manager is only too aware of how they are doing day to day, week to week, month to month. The pressure – when it's not going well – is intense, so I wanted to give some general advice of how to handle this and how to try to reverse the trend. These are a few pointers of what to consider:

- Don't be too stubborn about your views but don't lose all your conviction. Ideally, your conviction level should be around the 50 per cent level (where 0 per cent equals no conviction and 100 per cent means you are so convinced you would never change your view). Maintain conviction but keep your flexibility.

- Don't box yourself into a corner with your own views (e.g. everyone knows you hate mining shares to such an extent that you find it very difficult ever to buy them back). Always allow yourself an exit.

- Listen to advice from others about why you are not doing well with an open mind. Seek views from colleagues about what you are doing wrong. You must be prepared to take criticism.

- It is essential to keep an open mind to other points of view, particularly views on your main holdings that conflict with your own. You should never feel that you are the complete expert on a particular stock and no-one else's view counts. Evaluate honestly why you believe they are wrong and you are right. Know what 'wrong' looks like for your investments, i.e. why they might not succeed.

- Check whether you views are firmly agreed with the consensus and therefore more risky.

- Don't give up on your principles. Don't try something very different that you don't believe in.

- Put down on paper your 'start from scratch' portfolio and see how that differs from what you own.

- Put down on paper your twenty worst investments over the past six or twelve months and an honest explanation of why they went wrong. What are the lessons from this? What are common denominators? Think more about the downside risks of your positions.

- Work out whether you are deciding how your day is spent or letting events and others dictate you calendar. You should always allocate the bulk of your working days to tasks/events that you choose.

- Make sure that you are spending enough time on looking for new ideas rather than just monitoring what you own already. A portfolio with very few new holdings can become stale.

- If you don't use it, try using technical analysis as a cross check for your views.

- As well as examining your individual bets look at the shape of your portfolio and check that it reflects your conviction levels. Are your strongest conviction bets large enough? What are the characteristics of the tail of your portfolio? Check your portfolio for unintended bets.

- Don't put a defensive shell around yourself, become fatalistic that there is nothing you can do to improve things and cut yourself off from colleagues and clients.

- Finally, when it's going well again don't forget the bad days and believe that you can walk on water – you can't; I couldn't; no-one can.

&& When it's going well again don't forget the bad days 55

Twelve qualities that make a good portfolio manager

'The right temperament is more important than IQ'

'[Lloyd George] had that deep original instinct which peers through the surface of words and things – the vision which sees dimly but surely the other side of the brick wall or which follows the hunt two fields before the throng. Against this industry, learning, scholarship, eloquence, social influence, wealth, reputation, an ordered mind, plenty of pluck counted for less than nothing. It was the very gift which the products of Eton and Balliol had always lacked – the one blessing denied them by their fairy godmother, the one without which all other gifts are so frightfully cheapened. He had the 'seeing eye''

Churchill

I believe that there are twelve attributes that make a good portfolio manager:

1. 'The seeing eye'

Fund management is like chess and the best fund managers can see a couple of moves ahead of their competitors. They need to understand not just the immediate effects of a change but the secondary effects. For example, everyone can work out that a falling dollar against the pound is bad news for UK-based manufacturers exporting to the US. It's perhaps less obvious that it's good for UK clothes retailers (much of their product is imported from overseas and priced in dollars) or for a UK TV company (many of the expensive blockbuster films they buy are priced in dollars). A fund manager needs to be a good lateral thinker – thinking tangentially about the world. They need to be prepared to question what others take for granted. They should be able to spot attributes of companies that are out of favour today but may excite investors at some stage in the future. A good fund manager needs vision.

2. Temperament

Having the right temperament is extremely important and I believe it to be more important than IQ. Having a reasonable level of intelligence is obviously essential but being super intelligent without the right temperament is useless. A good fund manager needs to be calm and treat success and failure the same. For example, they mustn't let a good run of winners go to their head (nor get too depressed when they have a run of several poor investments). I think very emotional people generally make poor fund managers. Good fund managers should be humble (humility is an attribute that many portfolio managers lack) and happy to make mistakes: mistakes are an integral part of the job. It's an odds game and no one gets it right all the time. A good fund manager can handle mistakes and learn from them. They need to be open-minded and questioning. They also need application and perseverance; it's a job of remorseless intensity day in, day out, and it can't be turned off. It's a never-ending race that you can't tire of. Unlike many other jobs, it's not based on projects but rather a continuum, so stamina is important. It is constantly challenging and this intellectual challenge of pitting your wits against other intelligent managers trying to do the same thing and being able to see day-by-day how you are doing is both at times draining but also very stimulating.

3. Organised

A good fund manager is well organised. Because information often comes to them in an unstructured manner, a manager needs to be disciplined in how they go about their job. Because the job has no beginning or end, and because it is never possible to say you know everything about a particular company or industry, there is a need for structure and many inexperienced fund managers flounder because they are unorganised. A good fund manager will plan their day so they drive the agenda, otherwise it's very easy to let events take over. You need to devote some of the day to events but you mustn't let them occupy all the day. Also, if you are not careful, you can become mesmerised by your Reuters or Bloomberg screen, and end up spending hours watching them to little avail. Often my non-investment colleagues would ask me what's going on in the market that day and they were surprised when I said I hadn't yet looked.

A good part of the job is digesting information, which can be in a written form, electronic or voicemails as well as face-to-face formal and informal meetings. One needs structure to be able to accommodate this. I often had particular times of the day when I did certain activities (e.g. reading written research on the train, or listening to voicemail between face-to-face meetings or in a taxi) and most fund managers devise such a framework to their day. Prioritising one's time is essential.

4. Hunger for analysis

Fund managers like to know how things work. They don't want to know just conclusions, but they like to know the process used to get there. They want to know how results have been achieved for example, what is the process that leads from the light switch to the light bulb illuminating and how does the bulb work. I think all fund managers are intellectually curious. A fund manager is always questioning and always thinking. There is no substitute in investment for doing your own thinking and one must allow time for this. The process of growing most of Fidelity's fund managers internally, through our team of analysts, works well because we find that people who prove themselves as good analysts go on to make good fund managers.

A senior investment colleague of mine has a question he asks all prospective analysts or fund managers looking to join our investment team: 'How many plastic bags are there in the world?' He's not so interested in the answer, but in how the individual goes about trying to answer the question. A good analyst will start thinking about either the demand side: how many shoppers there are in the world, how many times they shop at how many shops, or at the supply side: how they are made, how many factories might there be in the world, what's the average output per factory etc..

5. A detailed generalist

A good fund manager needs to know a reasonable amount about the wide range of businesses and industries listed on the stock markets that they cover. Their knowledge needs to be both broad and also in reasonable depth in each area. They also need to be able to get up to speed quickly on a new subject so that, in a few hours of study, they become more knowledgeable than the average investor. Although they don't need to have the detailed knowledge that a specialist analyst would have on their own sector, it helps if they have reasonable knowledge of a comprehensive list of sectors and companies.

When I meet other successful fund managers, their wide knowledge, even about topics unrelated to the stock market, never fails to impress me.

6. Desire to win

Fund management is one of the most competitive jobs and unlike many other activities you see how you are doing day by day, even hour by hour or minute by minute. Jeremy Grantham puts it this way: 'The investment management business creates no value, but it costs, in round numbers, 1 per cent a year to play the game. In total, we are the market, and given costs, we, collectively, *must* underperform. It is like a poker game in which the good player must inflict his costs and his profits on to a loser. To win by 2 per cent, you must find a volunteer to lose by 4 per cent, every year ... Indexing must surely squeeze out active managers until it represents a substantial majority of the business. Remember, it is the worst player who drops out of the poker game to index. The standard of the remaining players, therefore, rises ... and rises ... but, fortunately for us, beginners continue to join the game.'

Fund managers need to be motivated to succeed in this intense and competitive environment.

7. Flexible conviction

Every fund manager needs conviction in their views, but they need what I call a flexible conviction or the ability to change their views if the evidence changes. In investment there is often a narrow line between certainty and uncertainty and to be too certain can be a disadvantage – one needs a continually open mind. Some cynicism is good but too much cynicism is a bad thing because the ultra-cynic will find a flaw in everything and never act. I don't think very cynical people make good investors. A good fund manager must avoid overconfidence or pig-headedness at all costs. If you are never prepared to change your mind you won't do well. Events happen often that cannot be predicted, and, if these negate one's investment thesis, one must be prepared to admit being wrong and move on.

> **“ A good fund manager must avoid overconfidence or pig-headedness at all costs ”**

8. Happy to go against the crowd

A good investment manager is 'their own man'; an independent thinker not over-influenced by, and often willing to challenge, conventional wisdom. Most importantly, they are happy to go against the crowd and they are not influenced by what the crowd is doing. Most human beings take comfort from the crowd and therefore contrarians are the exception rather than the rule. I'm often asked if it is something you are born with or whether you can learn to be a contrarian. I think it can be learnt but many contrarians are born that way.

Many of the best investments I've made have felt uncomfortable at the time I've made them (including my more successful market calls). Often by the time an investment is 'comfortable', particularly, in the recovery/turnaround field, it's too late. A good investor is not worried about what others think despite Keynes's observation that 'worldly wisdom teaches that it is better for the reputation to fail conventionally than to succeed unconventionally'.

9. Know yourself

A fund manger needs to know themselves, know their strengths and weaknesses and compensate for them. Also, I believe a good fund manager needs to find a style or method that suits their temperament and then stick to that approach. There are many approaches to making money in the stock market and the portfolio manager needs to be able to establish what works for them personally and then stick to it. I don't believe a manager can be a jack of all trades, switching between different approaches over time.

> **❝ Democracy does not make a good fund manager ❞**

Fund management is very much an individual activity. The final decisions are best made by individuals. Democracy does not make a good fund manager.

10. Experience

Beware of what John Train calls the 'Icarus syndrome' – 'nothing is more dangerous than trusting a young enthusiast who has done brilliantly for a while – what I call the Icarus syndrome. With a distressing fatality he plunges to earth in the next bear market ... I want to see a manager who has been tested by hard times, a veteran campaigner.' Experience is valuable. As Mark Twain put it, 'history never repeats itself, but it rhymes' – the same patterns do reoccur over time and one is not a 'seasoned' investor until one has

❝ History never repeats itself, but it rhymes ❞

experienced a full economic and stock market cycle. Being able to put today's events in a historical context is really useful.

Additionally, a good fund manager never stops learning – I didn't.

11. Integrity

Integrity is essential. Integrity is being honest with investors, companies and colleagues but, just as important, being honest with oneself.

12. Common sense

My final quality is perhaps such an obvious one it's surprising to be on the list but I do believe it is important and often under-appreciated. When presented with some-

❝ When it seems too good to be true it probably is ❞

thing new or unusual in an investment I always went back to first principles – does this make sense? It's amazing how often this stopped me doing something that I would later have very much regretted. When it seems too good to be true it probably is. When I came away from a company meeting saying I didn't understand why there is such a demand for a particular product, or I didn't understand how this worked, that was a warning – even though no one else appeared to make the same observation. For example, the first time someone explained a CPDO (constant proportion debt obligation) to me, one of the more risky and complex inventions of credit repackaging, I thought the product made no sense. I doubt after recent events we will ever see them issued again.

Many investors look for short cuts when investing as an easy option. There is absolutely no substitute for doing your own thinking.

Good fund managers come from a range of academic backgrounds. I don't believe that there is one type of qualification that is more appropriate for the job than others and a good fund manager needs both quantitative and qualitative attributes.

&& Every good manager will have an underperforming year &&

Most importantly remember when judging results, it is extremely difficult to differentiate between luck and judgement over short periods of time of, say, less than three-in-a-row years. Skilful investors need time for the probabilities to work in their favour. Every good manager will have an underperforming year – I had three, in 1989, 1990 and 1991!

Two

Experiences and reflections from a life running money

Some memorable company meetings

keep my company meeting notes in ruled A4 notebooks (I prefer notebooks to individual sheets of paper that can easily get lost over time). I started taking notes of my UK company meetings in 1987 and by the time I stopped running the Special Situations Fund I was on my fifty-second book (with just under 100 notes per book that's about 5,000 company meetings). Similarly, I did the same for European company meetings starting in 1985, the year Fidelity European Fund was launched, and have filled thirty-seven books.

There is a possible myth that such company notes are of great interest to the outside world. Looking back at these notes I find most today rather mundane and full of details that meant a lot at the time but are much less interesting years later. You need to remember that these notes were supplemental to all the other information we were studying at the time rather than being a self-contained overview of the company. Some of the most interesting meetings were those in my early days of investing in Europe (even before the European Fund was launched I was investing the Special Situations Fund in Europe). I describe some of these meetings below.

My first trip to see European companies was to Norway in November 1983. Norway has been an area of particular interest to me and somewhere where I have been able to find a lot of opportunities. I saw two companies during that first trip. One was Norsk Data, a manufacturer of medium-sized computers, and the other Norgas, an industrial gases company with a small pharmaceutical business specialising in contrast media (when injected into the body, contrast media make X-rays and scans clearer). Since then, each has had very different fortunes.

Norsk Data was a boom to bust growth stock. It did very well for a while and was a stock widely held by European fund managers. Later, the business matured as competition grew and started to decline eventually, I believe, going into liquidation. On the other hand, the pharmaceutical part of Norgas became Nycomed, which was one of Norway's great success stories making investors several times their initial investment. It was one of my top ten holdings in the Special Situations Fund in 1981 and again in 1984 and 1985. The company merged with the UK company Amersham in October 1997.

On that 1983 trip I also visited the chief investment officer of a large local insurance company. I remember asking him who did the best local research into Norwegian companies; 'Nobody in Oslo' was his answer. If I wanted research on Norwegian companies then he recommended I speak to Grieveson Grant in London (today part of Dresdner Kleinwort Benson). His comment reflected the fact that in many countries in Europe in those days there was very little local research being done. He was a serious man without much humour and I remember seeing him again on a subsequent trip. He asked me what companies I was visiting and I told him of several including a distributor of computing equipment, the management of which didn't impress me and which I thought was very speculative. I asked him what his views of the company were. He said it was very difficult for him to talk about the company because he was in fact a director! I soon learnt to keep my views to myself in a small community like Oslo.

I should have bought Ericsson shares after my first trip in October 1984. If I had, I would have made a lot of money. I remember I was put off by the telephone on the desk of the person I visited; it was one of the most old-fashioned devices I had ever seen. I thought how could a leading telephone company let its employees use such antiquated machines? Perhaps I should have been more impressed by Ericsson's ability to keep costs down.

It's interesting that in the 1980s, the way that we were received at European companies could vary from unfriendly at one end of the scale, to very welcoming at the other. Most companies, however, were generous with their time and information. Seeing investors was a novelty and the fact that somebody had actually flown over from the UK to spend time with them, and was interested in the detail of their company, meant they were very willing to spend hours discussing it. In some cases, they preferred talking to foreign investors because if they talked to a local one, or a local broker, information might end up in the newspapers. I'm sure a few times I heard more than I should have done. I remember once or twice they thought that as we were part owners they should share with us the management accounts and budgets. Occasionally, we were the first investor to visit the company, as was the case with a trip to Madrid in August 1989 to see the Spanish tobacco monopoly Tabacalera.

Some misunderstood our motivation for visiting them. I remember a trip to a small German property company where the managing director informed us when we arrived that he could only spare us about half an hour and anyway he couldn't understand why we wanted to meet him. After twenty minutes or so of questioning his whole attitude changed as he started to realise we knew quite a bit about his company and wanted to know more. In the end we stayed two and a half hours and he was happy to explain all about his property portfolio. His office floor ended up covered in maps and plans of buildings as he described each property the company owned in great detail.

Our general experience was that once we explained why we wanted to visit a company and the management realised that we already knew a lot about them they were happy to spend time with us. An exception in May 1988 was my first (and last) visit to the AP Møller companies in Denmark – the country's largest industrial group, being family controlled with a reputation for great secrecy. A London broker had managed to get me an appointment with the finance director. When I arrived, he asked: 'What have you come to sell me.' I said: 'Nothing, we're potential investors and I've come to learn more about your company.'

To which he replied: 'Well I'm sorry. Our policy is not to talk to investors.' I spent a pleasant half hour talking about Denmark and the world investment scene. Once or twice I tried to steer the conversation towards Møller's activities, but each time he deflected my enquiries. The visit was a write-off but there was a silver lining. In 1992, he changed jobs to become chief executive of another Danish company, the East Asiatic Company, and we subsequently had a number of meetings with him discussing his new company at length and built up an excellent relationship.

Other frustrations in those early days were companies with other agendas. The Italian food company in March 1985 that was more interested in persuading us to try their ice-cream than discussing the company; or the visit to German mortgage banks later that year when they fielded their head of securities wanting to pitch for our equity business rather than letting us learn about their own businesses.

I was lucky in December 1986 to go on one of the first investor trips to Portugal not long after the stock market was opened to foreign investors. The trip ended with a visit to the stock exchange, no bigger than a living room, where prices were set once or twice a day. Luckily, I also heard about a small conglomerate called Sonae whose interests included supermarkets. We were among its first foreign investors and the shares subsequently rose ten-fold.

In June 1987 (a few months before the stock market crash) I visited two Finnish conglomerates in Helsinki. One was Amer, which had activities that included car distribution, tobacco and paper manufacturing and engineering. It also had a small subsidiary making hockey sticks. Later, after taking over Wilson, the golf and tennis business, as well as Atomic, the ski business, it became a sporting goods company, selling everything else.

The other conglomerate we visited on that trip made a range of goods, such as paper, TV sets, tyres and even wellington boots.

My attention was caught by a division called Mobira, which was expanding its sales at 50 per cent a year. Over the next few years the company had a torrid time – it had a number of chief executives in short succession, several of whom didn't last longer than a year with the final one sadly committing suicide. In early 1992, the finance director was promoted to chief executive and in March 1993 he visited our London office. This was one of the most interesting and exciting meetings I have ever attended and I bought a lot of shares after the meeting. The chief executive's name was Jorma Ollila and the company was Nokia. At the meeting he told us that all the company's divisions except for Mobira, the mobile phone subsidiary, were likely to be sold. Interestingly, he told us that in 1989 Mobira had lost money and they weren't sure at the time whether it could be fixed! By 1993, things had completely changed and he said US sales were 'amazing' and he was very optimistic. Because up until then divisional profits had not been disclosed, we only realised for the first time at that meeting that big losses in their other consumer electronics businesses were hiding excellent profits in the mobile phone side, something not generally understood. The rest, as they say, is history.

In May 1992, Colin Stone, a colleague, and I visited a Finnish IT company then called TT Tieto. It was a computer services company with a dominant position in Finland and it specialised in taking over corporate and public sector IT departments and running them more efficiently. Coming out of the meeting, we said to each other almost simultaneously 'ten bagger' (a term Peter Lynch used to describe stocks that could go up ten times in value). We concluded that if the company was quoted elsewhere, the facilities management nature of the business with its recurring revenue would justify a much higher valuation, particularly as the accounting was very conservative with high depreciation and strong cash balances. Also, chief executive Matti Lehti thought the margins could increase from an average 4 per cent in the 1980s to 10 per cent. After the meeting we increased our holding to 15 per cent of the company (the maximum position we could take) and our share price prediction proved correct.

There were also a few visits that stopped me investing in, or persuaded me to sell out of, disasters. One was a visit to a German steel company in April 1990. I had a breakfast meeting with the finance director, throughout which he drank copious amount of *sect*, the local sparkling wine. I was very surprised at this behaviour and I didn't invest in the company. Later, I heard that the company was in difficulties. Another near miss was KHD, a German engineering company that I had arranged to visit with a British broker. We got as far as the reception only to be told they had a change of policy and had decided after all not to see prospective investors; the broker was extremely embarrassed. Although I wasn't very happy at the time as I had thought that the company might have been an interesting investment, I possibly had a fortunate escape as a few years later the company was in effective bankruptcy.

Perhaps one of the most dramatic visits I've done was one to Barcelona in 1988 to see the chief executive of a go-go Spanish conglomerate called Torras Hostench, which was one of my biggest holding in the Special Situations Fund at the time. One of its attractions was that the Kuwait Investment Office, who had interests in Spain at the time, had a large shareholding in the company (sovereign wealth funds are not a new phenomenon). The first person we met in reception was an armed bodyguard. We had a poor meeting with the chief executive that was constantly interrupted by him taking calls from a phone hidden below his desk. After our meeting he invited us to lunch; we got into his car as did two bodyguards and drove no more than fifty yards to the other side of a tree-lined boulevard. I sold the shares shortly thereafter – if he needed all those bodyguards, particularly for such a short journey, he probably wasn't to be trusted and had something to hide. The company later became one of the biggest Spanish bankruptcies and I believe he ended up in prison.

In 1994 I went to visit one of the most extraordinary companies I've ever come across – a Swiss newspaper company called NZZ. On paper, the shares looked extremely attractive selling at only 5 times cash flow and under book value. At the meeting I discovered that shares could only be owned by residents of the canton of Zurich and members of the Free Democratic Party. However, I was aware that some foreigners had bought shares in NZZ and I asked the director we were seeing what their position would be. He was quite clear; all rights remained with the seller. 'All rights?' I asked. 'Yes, all rights,' he replied, 'voting, dividends, scrip issues' – effectively the foreigners had bought nothing. Besides moving to Zurich and proving your democratic principles, you were prohibited from being a shareholder. I will do a lot to add an attractive stock to the fund but that was going a little too far!

In the 1980s and early 1990s Switzerland had a generally unreceptive approach to foreign shareholders. They were only allowed to buy non-voting certificates or, in a few cases, the companies assigned them bearer shares. As a result, many companies were not interested in meeting foreign institutional investors. An example was one of my holdings in the European Fund at the time, the travel company Kuoni. It was very restrictive in terms of giving out information and allowed us to visit once a year if we were lucky. One day, it was announced that a large shareholding in the company that had been held by a German retailer had been placed in the market and as a result we found the attitude completely changed – the protection of a large, friendly shareholder having been removed. They even sought our advice in terms of what we wanted from companies in which we had invested and how they should handle meetings. Subsequently, they provided much more financial information and agreed to meet or talk to us in Switzerland or the UK (they have a large UK subsidiary specialising in long-haul travel). The information showed that several divisions, including the UK, were doing very well but three or four others were in loss, so overall the profitability was below average. They explained to us their plans to eradicate these losses. The shares subsequently did very well.

The Swiss example of restricted voting rights was not unique. Across Europe there were still lots of examples of voting restrictions on different classes of shares as well as different shareholders having different rights. For example, in Italy, Germany and several other markets, if a majority owner sold its shares to a third party the minority shareholders didn't necessarily get the same price. In 1995, I wrote in a speech about investing in Europe: 'Germany still ranks at the bottom of the European league in terms of shareholder friendliness. Here, almost uniquely in Europe today, we find companies that refuse to see us even though we are shareholders. These are companies such as Otto Reichelt, a Berlin-based food retailer; Villeroy & Boch, a building materials company; Axel Springer, the newspaper company; and Altana, the drug company. Another aspect of the German approach is that many companies are floated with only preference shares quoted on the market. These carry no votes and presumably the management feel extra secure knowing outside shareholders can never have any influence on the company – unless the preference dividends are not paid. Holland has a different structure where in some cases managing boards are voted in by supervisory boards and supervisory boards by management boards, a completely circular structure over which poor shareholders can have very little influence. This had led to instances of one company owning a majority of shares in another but having no control over it. Also, companies are generally allowed three forms of protection from unwarranted take-overs.' I remember discussing this practice with a board member of a poorly performing Dutch company. 'Why three?' I asked. 'Surely one or at most two would be enough?' 'We're allowed three so we've got three,' was his reply. I mentioned that some companies had four – four he thought was unreasonable! Things have progressed in Germany, Switzerland and Holland since those days, although today it is some of the Mediterranean countries that lag behind the rest of Europe.

Two of the more unusual companies I used to go to visit were Société des Bain de Mer in Monte Carlo and Astra in Luxembourg. Société des Bain de Mer owned many of the hotels, casinos and shops in Monte Carlo and even some of the roads; the majority of its shares were held by the prince of Monaco. For a long time the company was not widely followed and the shares sold on a very low valuation. It always surprised me that more investors didn't visit them as Monte Carlo is hardly the worst place to go!

Astra owns the satellites that broadcast programmes across Europe for a number of satellite TV stations, including Sky. I will never forget the approach to their office, driving across green rolling countryside when, almost out of nowhere, towering above the trees you suddenly see the huge space-age domes of their transmitters, which beam the programmes up to the satellites miles above the earth. One thing that I learnt particularly sticks in my mind about my early discussions with the finance director. I remember him telling me that he was really scared whenever they launched a satellite and I asked why this was. He told me that at the time it was too expensive to insure the satellites against launch failure, which was a real risk. If the launch went wrong, a one in six chance, millions of francs could disappear in a few minutes.

It's interesting that in those days analysts could even get a basic statistic about a company wrong, such as the number of shares outstanding. I remember going to visit Arbed, the Luxembourg-based steel company, in November 1988. The finance director was very helpful and answered all our questions fully. We found out that analysts had overestimated the total diluted number of shares as the company had bought in an outstanding convertible. Also, a Belgium steel associate, thought only to be 30 per cent owned, was in fact over 50 per cent owned through other subsidiaries. So the facts weren't understood and adjusting for these we had a company selling for only 4 times consolidated earnings, 1.5 times consolidated cash flow and at over a 50 per cent discount to book, a large discount to any other European steel company valuation. We added to our holding.

We made a lot of money investing in commercial television shares in Europe in those days. We were able to take our knowledge of investing in television in the more developed UK market into Europe, where commercial stations were in their infancy. We did well in companies such as TF1 in France, Antena TV in Spain as well as investing in German, Dutch, Italian, Swedish and Norwegian companies that had commercial television interests. Industries develop at different paces in different countries, and having the knowledge of an advanced country can put one ahead of the crowd in a less developed one. One particular opportunity sticks out. In April 1996 I went to Helsinki and saw MTV, which was the only commercial television company broadcasting in Finland at the time. Like most other European markets, the state-owned channels were the main broadcasters but they were not run to make money and being the first commercial station was normally an excellent opportunity. The shares were not listed but they were quite widely owned, mainly by other Finnish companies, and did change hands. I don't remember the exact valuation but the shares traded on only 4 times or 5 times earnings. I asked how we could buy shares. I was told that every new shareholder had to be approved by the board. Luckily, the chairman of the board was none other than Jorma Ollila, chief executive of Nokia, whom by then we knew quite well. When I got back to London I called him and told him of our interest in the company. He said he would be delighted to approve Fidelity as a shareholder. Eventually the company was taken over by a local newspaper group.

One visit in June 1994 made a particular impression for an unusual reason. This was to the head office on the outskirts of Paris of Guilbert, a small office supplies distributor with a good track record. When we entered the reception area I saw a large board with Guilbert's share price displayed on it. This would have been quite a common practice in the US at the time and occasionally you saw it in the UK, but it was the first time I had seen it in Europe. I was impressed that this company was so focused on its share price and it was one of the reasons that I bought the shares after the visit.

In the late 1990s European companies started coming to London much more regularly to visit their investors and most of our meetings used to take place in our offices in the City. It was a more efficient use of my time to see the companies in our offices than going out all over Europe to visit them, although it was in some ways less interesting.

I think the first UK company visit I went on was in the 1970s when I was working in my first job at Keyser Ullmann, the merchant bank. It was to a small Welsh company called EC Cases, which manufactured pots and pans and other metal household items. After meeting with the management we were given a tour of the factory and straight away noticed a huge pile of boxes at one end of the building. When we asked what they were, we were told that they were returned saucepans. Apparently there was a design fault and the handles weren't well insulated so that, when the pan was on the hob, the handle heated up as much as the pan! As soon as we got back to the office we sold all the shares that we held.

The first meeting in my UK notebook was on June 24, 1987 with ERF, a commercial vehicle manufacturer. Not long afterwards I had a meeting on July 7 with the chairman of Mersey Docks. The company owned the docks in Liverpool and was one of my best investments. It was a recovery stock, which had very strong asset backing in the form of commercial property and during the time Special Situations owned the shares they went up tenfold.

One of the more unusual UK companies I visited was Paterson Zochonis (now called PZ Cussons). This was a Manchester-based company that had its origins as a trading company in Nigeria. Later, it shifted its focus to manufacturing and as well as factories in Nigeria it developed plants in Thailand, Indonesia, Kenya, Greece and Poland making detergents, cosmetics, soaps and edible oils. It also owned Cussons, whose products included Imperial Leather soap and it had a large investment portfolio of equities, bonds and bank deposits. There were two classes of shares; one with votes and one without, and the family controlled 65 per cent of the voting shares. As a family controlled company it didn't hold many meetings with investors but in May 1994 the company's official broker managed to get me a meeting in Manchester with the finance director. It was a very good meeting and I learnt a lot about the company. I didn't buy the shares at that time because I think I was concerned about the outlook for their Nigerian businesses. However, three years later, the same finance director and also the chairman came to visit us in London and I subsequently bought a holding. The shares had been very lowly valued, particularly if the cash and securities on their balance sheet were taken into account. On the back of their success in raising profits and the increasing interest from investors in emerging markets the shares performed very well over the next few years and were substantially revalued.

Drug companies are generally considered to be safe investments, particularly as they are insulated from the effects of an economic downturn. Therefore, I was particularly surprised when during a meeting with Glaxo in May 1988 a director described the business as being 'very risky' (he was perhaps one of the more sincere directors I've met). His point was that the top ten selling drugs at the time were different from the top ten years earlier. Although the immediate future was rosy because of the launch of Zantac (which at the time was the world's biggest selling prescription drug) he didn't seem confident about replacing the top sellers again over the next ten years, even though £500m had just been spent on a research centre in Stevenage; twenty years on his observation seems as true as ever.

I want to end this section with a discussion of two of my biggest mistakes during the early 1990's and one company that, despite becoming over-geared, survived and subsequently proved an excellent investment and is in FTSE 100 today.

I visited Azil Nadir's first listed company, Wearwell, at their office near Commercial Road in the 1980's. Subsequently he bought into a small 'shell' company called Polly Peck and I started buying shares in the late 1980's. It was one of my top ten holdings in 1987, 1988 and 1989. Initially, the business was focused on the export and packing of fruits from northern Cyprus, but later it built up a much wider selection of interests including electronics and hotels in Turkey, as well as global food and shipping operations, and eventually became a FTSE 100 company. Before the shares were suspended in September 1990 there were some warning signs, including very high margins versus peers and a growing amount of debt. Also that year, the management had tried to do an MBO of the business, but didn't succeed. I remember as we sat in his smart Berkeley Square offices in 1990, surrounded by antique rugs and cabinets, sipping orange juice and discussing his business. Azil Nadir came across as cultured and refined – as well as being very believable. The group finances eventually became overstretched and there were questions about the level of margins in the business. Aspects of the company were subsequently investigated by the Serious Fraud Office.

Another mistake of this period was a conglomerate called Parkfield. The company which had been built up by acquisitions had interests in foundries, aluminium wheels for cars, video tape distribution and film ownership. Its chief executive was called Roger Felber. The company was first highlighted to me by a

Midlands based broker and I think that the first time I met Mr Felber was at an institutional lunch they organised with him. Subsequently we had some very good meetings with the company, where they gave us lots of information on the different subsidiaries, and following meetings in September 1988 I started to purchase shares in February 1989. By early 1990 it had become one of my top 10 holdings and there were reports of financial difficulties at the company. I thought we needed a further meeting to investigate this and we arranged to visit their head office in Haslemere, Surrey. Since the early 1980's I have lived nearby and commuted daily by train from Haslemere to London. This meeting was the only meeting that I've ever done with a company in Haslemere and it's ironic that it should have been a company that later went into receivership. My assistant at the time – a very able lady analyst who had moved to London from our Boston office – and I spent a couple of hours there. The finance director was very reassuring about the company's finances and here was such an atmosphere of calm and business as usual at their headquarters that we both returned to London believing the reports false. I couldn't believe that within a few months the shares would be suspended and effectively worthless; a huge build up in working capital in the video distribution business was one of the main contributing factors.

The episode has a postscript: A few years later we were looking to move house in the area and we were taken by our agent to a large period property. It was very impressive and I asked the agent who the seller was: 'What's his name?' I asked.

'Mr Felber' was the reply 'why do you know him?'

Both Polly Peck and Parkfield had poor balance sheets, perhaps not initially, but certainly in their later stages, although our analysis didn't identify this at the time. It was this experience, and some other bankruptcies in the portfolio at the time such as Mountleigh, Doctus, Babcock Prebon and Merlin Properties, that became the reason I vowed from then on only to invest in companies that had weak balance sheets with my eyes fully open. We also had to have better ways of identifying companies whose balance sheets were stretched.

The third company that brought home to me the importance of balance sheets was WPP. I met Martin Sorrell when he was finance director of Saatchi and Saatchi. In 1985, he bought into a cash shell called Wire and Plastic Products and used the shell to make acquisitions in the advertising and media area. These were often partially financed via earnouts (part of the acquisition price was payable in later years depending on the acquisition's profit record). These acquisitions included the J. Walter Thompson Group in 1987 for $566m and the Ogilvy Group for $864m in 1989. This latter purchase, mainly financed with debt, was the deal too far that caused problems later on. I held shares on and off in the late 1980s and my first notes of a meeting were in March 1988. The recession of the early 1990s started to affect WWP's trading as many companies cut their media spending. This was particularly the case in late 1991 when the group had debt of £450m, which rose above £500m at seasonal peaks.

In May 1992, some prominent bankers came to see us and several other larger shareholders with a proposal to change the management and inject £100m of new equity into the business. I had a holding at the time but WPP was not one of my larger holdings because I was expecting a refinancing of some sort. I was enthusiastic, but because of the precarious nature of the company's finances and the fact that the main businesses were in the US I asked a unit in our Boston office that specialised in refinancing to review the situation. They looked at the proposals and the new management team in great detail and concluded that the status quo was the best option. Shortly after, WPP itself approached us with its own restructuring plan, which involved raising new equity in the form of convertible preference shares and converting part of the bank debt into such shares. We initially thought that the conversion terms were too generous to the banks and until very late in the day we tried to get the company to revise the terms. Unfortunately, we were not successful and finally accepted the proposals reluctantly.

With the finances fixed, WPP became a great recovery candidate. I held shares continuously from 1991 to 1997 and in 1993, 1994 and 1995, WPP was one of my top ten holdings; it did very well under Sorrell's able and long-standing leadership. The shares joined the FTSE 100 in 1998 and Martin Sorrell today is one of the longest standing FTSE 100 chief executives. Most chief executives don't survive a refinancing, as happened to WPP in the early 1990s. He's the exception.

chapter

19

Some of my best *and worst* investments

have detailed performance attribution figures only for the last eight years that I ran the Special Situations Fund. I will discuss some of the best and worst investments over that period as well as a few of the stocks that really helped or hindered me before then. These are summarised in Table 1 at the end of this chapter.

My ten best performers from 2000 to 2007 were: Autonomy, ICAP, Gallaher Group, Cairn Energy, MMO2, Amlin, Balfour Beatty, George Wimpey, BG Group and Safeway. My ten worst were: Sportingbet, Rank Group, ITV, GCAP Media, SMG, Premier Foods, Isoft, Cookson Group, SSL Intl., British-Borneo Oil & Gas.

It's ironic that one of my best stocks over the last seven years of running the fund was Autonomy, a stock in the vanguard of the technology-media-telecoms (TMT) bubble. I remember asking my colleague Colin Stone, who ran some of our growth funds, that if I wanted to own one new economy stock, which should I choose. He suggested Autonomy, which was one of his big positions. I guess the cleverest thing I did was to sell it at the right time before the bubble had fully burst.

My second biggest contributor was ICAP. I had followed the money-broking business since the 1980s and had been a holder in Exco, Mills & Allen and a small broking business, Trio, in the 1990s. In October 1998 Michael Spencer's private broking operations made a successful reverse takeover for Exco and in September 1999 this group, then called Intercapital, merged with another broker called Garban. Garban was originally owned by the media company Mills & Allen (later after a merger Mills and Allen became United Business Media). In November 1998, to focus on the media industry, United Business Media spun off their money-broking business to shareholders. Initially the shares were very lowly valued. I made it a reasonably-sized position in the fund and by 2001 it was one of my biggest holdings. Later it changed its name to ICAP. It was one of the first brokers to exploit the benefits of electronic broking (before then, broking was done on the telephone). This strategy proved hugely successful as well as expanding the range of products it brokered. It entered FTSE 100 in 2006.

Tobacco shares have been strongly re-rated in this decade. Investors have been attracted by the receding threat of litigation in the US, steady earnings growth, particularly from emerging markets, and the potential for M&A. Gallagher had always been one of my favourite tobacco companies because of its interesting geographic exposure and its attractions as a bid candidate, and I first purchased shares in the late 1990s. It was eventually bought by Japan Tobacco in December 2006 although, by then, I had already taken my profits. Today, the sector is valued at a premium to others rather than the discount at which it sold for many years. As the anti-smoking lobby grows and eventually affects the growth of the business, even in emerging markets, investors may well reassess the companies and return them to lower relative valuations.

I did well out of the oil exploration company Cairn Energy in the mid-1990s when it discovered oil and gas in a number of places including Bangladesh. I was fortunate to sell in 1997 when the shares were high. Unfortunately, some of its finds did not live up to expectations and the shares fell back. In 2000, I started accumulating the shares again when they were much lower. The company kindly provided the data to compile the history in Figure 1, which shows Fidelity's holdings between February 1994 and October 2003.

I always rated the management team highly. The chief executive has an attractive strategy of balancing low risk wells and producing assets, which provided cash flow, with big stakes in higher-risk exploration interests, which if successful would really make shareholders a lot of money. Such an asset was their onshore interests in Rajasthan in India. In 2004 they purchased a

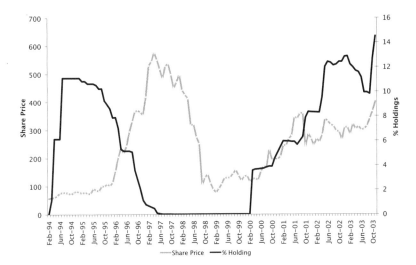

Figure 1. Fidelity's holdings in Cairn Energy

50 per cent interest in this area from Shell for only about £7m (this must go down as one of the worst deals done by a major oil company) and have since made a number of finds there. Today, this area is valued at around £3bn. Cairn Energy went into the FTSE 100 on the back of these finds and has floated a minority of the shares of the company that owns its Indian interests on the Indian stock market. The chief executive recently told me that original investors in Cairn have made 100 times their money – very few companies can beat that.

I mentioned MMO2 in the chapter on M&A as an example of a company that was always likely to be bought by a larger telecoms company (as the chief executive told us at our first meeting.) It is also an example of the attractions of spin-off companies. In November 2001, MMO2 was spun off from BT and all BT shareholders received shares in MMO2. However, as it was a substantially smaller company, many BT shareholders decided to sell the shares rather than hold what for many must have been a very small holding. This initial selling presented us an attractive opportunity. As with many companies that start as divisions of much larger companies but break away, the management was incentivised by the prospect of running the company and owning shares in it. I remember the chief executive saying that they should be able to improve the financial performance of the business substantially by increasing margins and revenue growth. He fully delivered on this promise.

In fact, this same mobile telephone business did very well for the fund in earlier years. A minority stake in the business, which was called Cellnet in those days, was owned by two listed sister businesses, Security Services and Securicor, before BT bought out this minority interest in 1999. I was very attracted to these businesses because I believed the value of their interest in Cellnet was not fully reflected in their own valuations. My holdings in these two businesses were the biggest holding in the Special Situations Fund in 1990, 1993, 1994, 1995 and 1996 and were a major contributor to the performance of the fund in those days. No other companies have appeared so regularly as my biggest holdings. It seems the only time I didn't make money out of it was when BT owned the business. I believe it was a strategic mistake for BT to have sold it (although debt pressures didn't give them much option.)

Amlin has been one of the most successful insurance companies at Lloyds. I became interested in this area in the late 1990s when companies were floated with the aim of providing corporate capital to Lloyd's. Initially, many of them invested in syndicates run by different managing agents, but over time most of them purchased managing agents and aligned the capacity they owned to the capacity managed by that agency or agencies. The advent of these vehicles led to a change in the way the Lloyd's market was financed with the majority of capacity at Lloyd's now owned by these vehicles and other corporate members rather that the individuals (Names) who used to provide all the capital. I have to admit my long-term experience of investing at Lloyd's has been a very up and down one. From the early days (my first holdings were in 1995), I purchased a number of companies as, from the outside, it was difficult to decide which would be the good performers and which would not be. Along the way, several of my holdings had difficulties, including Goshawk, SVB and Cox Insurance. Also, when disasters occurred such as the attacks on the US in 2001, or the hurricanes in 2005, the stocks performed very poorly shortly afterwards and a number subsequently needed more capital, although these disasters were often the precursor of more favourable underwriting conditions. The longer I invested, the less keen I was on the business model, particularly those companies only exposed to Lloyd's which, I believe still needs to make changes to the way it operates (such as aligning capacity on its syndicates and voting power). Also, capital moves much more freely these days and when underwriting conditions are favourable new capital can quickly come into the market. I met Charles Philipps in September 1997 when he was finance director of Angerstein Underwriting. He subsequently became chief executive of Amlin and has made the company one of the leaders at Lloyd's as well as starting insurance operations in Bermuda. In an industry where companies are often tempted to under-provide for future losses, Amlin has always been an example of prudence and good underwriting practices. The long-term performance of the shares has been excellent.

My worst investment during the seven-year period was Sportingbet. Much has been written about the demise of companies such as Sportingbet and PartyGaming. I knew I was investing in a company with an above-average level of risk because of the questions surrounding the legality of online betting in the US. That said, we talked to many legal experts and they all agreed, before the event, that what eventually happened in the US was extremely unlikely to happen. A law was introduced outlawing the payment for internet gambling by tagging it on to another bill to do with US port legislation at the eleventh hour. Although I was upset that our advisers had been so wrong, when buying risky stocks one must expect from time to time the odds to go sour. I feel sure that online gambling will be legalised eventually in the US and when that happens US gambling companies will be able to dominate the business, because the UK competition has been conveniently eradicated.

For many years Rank Group was, in my view, a poorly run business with too wide a range of activities under a broad leisure heading. However, more recently I felt it was a prime beneficiary from gambling deregulation in the UK. As well as its bingo operations it owns one of the biggest casino businesses in the UK (I've always liked casino businesses with their ability to generate cash). I was probably too slow to realise how big a U-turn the government made in regard to gambling deregulation and also the company was more badly affected by the smoking ban in bingo halls than we first thought. The other reason I kept the share was the new chief executive Ian Burke was particularly impressive and the company was a prime bid target.

I have been a long-term fan of the UK broadcasting sector. From 1986 until 1999 (when the TMT boom raised valuations too high) the fund always held some holdings in TV companies. Also from 1991 to 1999 I held Capital Radio. Generally, the performance of these shares was very good. Although these businesses have been affected this decade by technological change and increased competition, I remain of the view that, if well run, their franchises remain valuable. However, I have been too optimistic in recent years about several media stocks, in particular ITV, GCAP and SMG. SMG (which owns Scottish TV and owned Virgin Radio until 2008) had the added problem of a weak balance sheet and a poor management track record. I often ask myself did I get too close to ITV over the period Fidelity was closely involved in changing the management (when I earned that awful nickname of 'the Silent Assassin')? Perhaps I did, although it did not stop me selling all my ITV shares when BSkyB bought its stake in 2006. That year it was one of my best performing shares after poor performance in 2004 and 2005. I bought back half the holding I sold to BSkyB and it again became a poor performer in 2007. I still believe, even in a fragmenting media environment, that the channels that can deliver the largest audiences to advertisers are attractive, but it was undoubtedly poorly run for many years and the programming could have been better. I continue to believe that with the right management, which it may now have (although we were not involved in the choice of Sir Michael Grade), it could do much better, especially if it's able to get contracts right renewal (CRR) altered or removed.

I think of all the stocks I have got wrong recently GCAP is perhaps the biggest disappointment. I am a great believer in radio, even in an online world, and audience figures (unlike TV) are not eroding. I am sorry Kate Haslett may not get a chance to run the group as a listed company as I believe she has the vision and charisma to reverse the company's recent poor financial performance.

Premier Foods became highly indebted after the acquisition of RHM in December 2006. I was always impressed with what management had achieved at the company from its initial flotation in July 2004. Also, I believe that food price inflation, should after a lag, be favourable for profitability. However, a stockbroker I have known for very many years implored me to sell the shares in 2007 because of their high debt levels and I wish I had taken his advice and not gone against my own advice about weak balance sheets.

Isoft was initially a beguiling story – a small UK software company that had won part of one of the largest IT contracts awarded in the UK or globally, in competition with some of the giants in the industry. The shares did well for a while helped by a persuasive managing director and some aggressive accounting of software revenues (which we initially didn't spot). I always expected Isoft in the long run to be bought by one of the big soft-ware names. In the end, a deteriorating balance sheet and delays in its software development programme led to it being forced to put itself up for sale. The price paid was a fraction of earlier valuations.

Besides the shares that have hurt me during the last seven years my performance was affected by not owning enough mining shares, particularly Xstrata, BHP Billiton and Anglo American. I have always had a bias against resource shares as I believe a big factor in their performance is the success or failure of their rel-evant commodities. I have always suggested that we generally have little competitive advantage in predicting commodity prices. I would rather invest in a company where I believe our bottom-up analysis gives us a bigger competitive advantage. In recent years I have also been influenced by the views of com-mentators such as Bill Miller at Legg Mason who argues that all commodity prices must over time return to the marginal cost of production – well below their levels at the time of writing. Commodity prices also have now been going up for some time and even in a world where there are inflationary threats I don't believe the demand for commodities is necessarily improving. Indeed, it is probably deteriorating with the slowdown in the west and the hording of commodities by China in the run-up to the 2008 Olympics. Commodity demand is often influenced by infrastructure spend more than consumption spend and I believe infrastructure spend is particularly sensitive to a credit tight-ening. However, one commodity I have been more attracted to is platinum and I have owned Lonrho, Impala Platinum and Aquarius Platinum in recent years. Here, a few suppliers domi-nate supply and have an influence on the market seen in few other commodities.

I've done very well investing in British Land shares and met them many times. Most recently, meetings have been with Stephen Hester, a very able chief executive. It is the only share to appear in my top holdings both in the very early days of my fund, 1981, and again more recently, 2005 – twenty-four years later! In recent years I did well investing in the large UK property stocks in the period up until the formation of UK REITs (real estate investment trusts). The journey often being better than the arrival from a stock market perspective, I substantially reduced my holdings towards the end of 2006. I did start building up again the holding in British Land towards the end of 2007 just before I gave up running the fund and after share prices had fallen back sharply. I will be interested to see whether this proves to be another good entry point or whether I was too early.

Finally, I would like to mention two other successes, Standard Chartered Bank and ED&F Man.

Standard Chartered Bank was in my top ten holdings in 2004, 2005, 2006 and much of 2007. I was attracted by its exposure to emerging markets, particularly in Asia and its good management team. I thought in the long run that its unique assets would eventually make it very attractive to a larger bank, while in the shorter term one benefited from exposure in a UK-listed company to some of the fastest growing economies in Asia and Africa.

I first bought ED&F Man in 1995 not long after its flotation and in 1997, 1998 and 1999 it was one of my largest holdings. When this business was floated it was mainly a commodity trading, sourcing and processing business with a very small financial side. The valuation of the business was very low. Over time the management changed the business mix, selling most of the commodity-related businesses by 2000 and expanding financial services. They bought interests in investment management companies running hedge funds. They themselves ran hedge funds and other funds, including an extraordinarily successful quantitative trading fund – AHL. Today, Man Investments is a global leader in alternative investments. The success of this strategy has led to a revaluation of the business, which has been a FTSE 100 constituent now for several years. I did very well in the early years but sold out too early. One reason was my concern at the sustainability of the AHL results, a concern that has proved incorrect to date.

Table 1. Contribution to net return through active bets

Year	Best	Worst
2000	Autonomy	Merant
	Celltech	British-Borneo Oil
	Reed International	Enodis
	Safeway	Compel
	Johnson Matthey	Scotia Holdings
	Ellis & Everard	Albert Fisher
	Gallaher Group	Allied Leisure
	Bank of Ireland	Cookson Group
	Wembley	
	Iceland Group	
2001	ICAP	Railtrack
	London Stock Exchange	Carlton Communications
	Arcadia	Iceland Group
	Inchcape	Novar
	Balfour Beatty	Enodis
	Safeway	Elementis
	George Wimpey	4 Imprint Group
	De Beers	SVB Holdings
	Gallaher	British Airways
	Carillion	Laird Group
2002	Credit Lyonnais	British Energy
	Harmony Gold	Cable & Wireless
	Gallaher Group	SSL Intl
	Amlin	Big Food Group
	Enterprise Oil	Bulmer HP
	MMO2	Cadiz Inc

-

	Bank of Ireland	Royal & Sun Alliance
	SOCO International	Carlton Communications
	George Wimpey	Oxford Glycosciences
	Kiln	Cookson Group
2003	Cable & Wireless	Goshawk Insurance
	Big Food Group	SOCO Intl
	WS Atkins	Tullow Oil
	NTL	Kiln
	Carlton Communications	Hiscox
	William Hill	Wellington U/W
	MMO2	Manangement Consultancy
	Mothercare	Beazley Group
	Somerfield	De la Rue
	Body Shop	Tenon
2004	Cairn Energy	ITV
	MMO2	Rank Group
	Celltech	Proteome Sciences
	London Stock Exchange	BG Group
	Carlton Communications	Big Food Group
	First Calgary Peteroleum	Aquarius Platinum
	Pendragon	Royal & Sun Alliance
	Allied Irish Banks	Reuters
	Orkla	Shire
	Land Securities	NTL
2005	Cairn Energy	GCap Media
	BG Group	ITV
	Statoil	William Hill
	Amlin	Marconi Corp
	British Energy	London Stock Exchange
	Roche	NTL
	Standard Chartered	Provident Financial
	C&C Group	SMG
	P&O Nedlloyd	Minerva
	SOCO Intl	Asia Energy

2006	ITV	Sportingbet
	Microfocus	Isoft
	British Land	Rank Group
	Mecom	GCap Media
	Expro International	BSkyB
	Shire	Reed Elsevier
	BG Group	Highland Gold
	Amlin	888 Holdings
	Astra Zeneca	SMG
	British Energy	Asia Energy
2007	Bayer	Premier Foods
	BG Group	Rank Group
	Electricité de France	GCap Media
	Nokia	Premier Farnell
	Reuters	SMG
	J Sainsbury	BP
	Reed Elsevier	British Land
	Xansa	Johnson Services Group
	Statoil Hydro	Erinaceous Group
	Vodafone	ITV

2000–2007	Autonomy	Sportingbet
	ICAP	Rank Group
	Gallaher Group	ITV
	Cairn Energy	GCAP Media
	MMO2	SMG
	Amlin	Premier Foods
	Balfour Beatty	Isoft
	George Wimpey	Cookson Group
	BG Group	SSL Intl
	Safeway	British-Borneo Oil & Gas

How the industry has changed

The City of London I joined in 1971 and the City today could not be more different. The City in the 1970s was a place of relatively short working hours (at least compared with today's long hours), long lunches where alcohol was usually consumed. It was nearly always the case that who you knew was as important as what you knew: many jobs were still awarded based on connections rather than ability. People worried about whether your shoes had laces and whether your shirt collar was stiff and detachable. The punishment for entering the stock exchange floor, if you were not a member and were caught out, was a public debagging (this was before women members were allowed). I remember a broker friend taking me on to the exchange floor illegally in the early 1970s, luckily without me being found out. When I started my first job at Keyser Ullmann in 1971, I spent the initial few weeks as a messenger delivering mail around the City by hand. It was thought a good way for me to learn where the most important buildings were (I don't think this has been much help particularly as many institutions have moved offices several times over my career).

As part of my training I also spent time in the money market department where representatives of the banks still used to visit each other wearing top hats. Every week we took part in the Bank of England tender for Treasury bills of three months' duration. I remember one time, when the directors took a long while to decide at what price to tender, I had to rush round to the Bank of England to get our tender in on time. As I entered the Bank, and because time was short, I started running down the long corridor which led to the window where the tenders had to be delivered before the noon deadline. Suddenly a voice rang out: 'Young man, no running in the Bank of England.' It was one of the Bank's messengers dressed in a pink morning suit who barred my way. When I finally got to the window the clerk told me he couldn't accept the tender because I'd folded the application form incorrectly – a tender was only acceptable if the piece of paper was folded exactly as the guidelines suggested! I don't think I was popular when I returned to our office having failed to get the tender in on time. Of course, this system disappeared a long time ago, as did the floor of the stock exchange. Nowadays, such processes are done electronically, more efficiently no doubt, but totally impersonal.

Two of the most significant changes in the investment industry have been the application of computers and the growth of available information. When I started, the standard calculator was about an A4-page size and plugged into the mains. Personal computers appeared in the early 1980s and I remember one of my colleagues requesting one. His boss was very reluctant to let him have one as he couldn't understand why he needed it. It is almost impossible to think of an era before spreadsheets, when P&L and balance sheet projections had to be copied out long hand and added up with a calculator. Similarly, all financial ratios such as PEs, yields and return on capital were worked out using calculators. Discounted cash flow models were hugely complex with the tools available at the time. Hand-in-hand with the growth of processing power has been the growth of information. Companies give out far more information today than they used to – more regularly and in far greater detail. Also, the number of reports published by brokers has multiplied many times (as has the number of brokers producing research across Europe). In my early years in investment management, the job was as much about trying to collect information others didn't have access to as it was about interpreting data and information. Today, it's the opposite. In the 1980s and 1990s our competitive edge came from having a much better information gathering system than our competitors. I remember going to visit companies in their offices and coming out thinking that I probably knew more about the company in question at that moment than any other investor, most of whom never got a chance to visit the company. In those days, European companies in particular gave out little official data – it was infrequent, often delayed and rarely in English. It was a huge advantage to have superior information and the task of outperforming competitors was easier particularly as there also was far less broker research then to help institutions who did not do their own research. Little original broker research was being done in continental Europe in the early 1980s (France and Germany were perhaps the exceptions) and experts, where they existed on areas such as Scandinavia and Spain, were normally in London.

When I left university and decided to join the City, investment management was not a popular career. My contemporaries who went into the City mainly chose corporate finance, which was the 'in' job in those days. Investment management had a low profile (for example, I knew very little about it until I started my first job). The tradition in the banks that had investment departments was that it was often considered an area that you went through before going on to do something much more important like running the bank itself. Investment was mainly about looking after private clients and a few institutional accounts such as insurance companies or pension funds. It may sound amazing, but performance measurement was in its infancy and often not considered at all. There was a view that just being able to pick shares and handle the process of buying or selling was a worthwhile skill in itself, regardless of whether one did it well or badly! The concept of beating the market or average was just starting to come in. Index funds were relatively unknown in the UK in the 1970s, although a small broker, Rowe Rudd, got a following in the late 1970s by being one of the first firms to write about index funds and the efficient market hypothesis. They were way ahead of their time; the idea of an indexed core to a portfolio is commonplace today, particularly for large funds.

In those days, investment management companies didn't do much of their own research, relying on broker research where available and broker recommendations (often not much more than tips or indications of what other investors were doing – confidentiality of trading not being a strong point in those days). Occasionally, there might be the chance to meet the management team at a group lunch. When European companies first came to London they would sit at one table, investors at another and maybe over coffee there would be a quick talk followed by perhaps two or three questions from the investors. Broker research went to all clients, although the rules were not as strict as today (actually, there were no rules) about everyone getting it at the same time so there was ample opportunity to front-run.

Generally, except at some merchant banks, there were no trading desks or dealing departments so each fund manager did his own buying and selling. This took up a reasonable part of the day, talking to brokers on the phone, discussing trends and giving out orders and receiving execution reports. Also, in those days one could buy shares, keep the bargain open sometimes for one or two days, see which way the trade went and then decide which account to allocate it to. It was not unheard of for banks to allocate successful trades to the bank's own account – or even to their employees' own personal accounts – and the unsuccessful ones to clients! Fortunately, such practices were stamped out long ago.

There were no Reuters or Bloomberg screens and the first system I remember seeing was the London Stock Exchange's own pricing system. Of course, the information was basic, only prices and news items, there being no ability to manipulate data or access other sources. Every contract note for every share bargain had to be checked by hand and it was not uncommon for directors or fund managers to have to sign every contract note to indicate that it was correct. Even in my early years at Fidelity I used to do this (eventually, I think I used a rubber stamp with my signature on it to make the signing of lots of notes quicker).

There was little interaction between the equity and the fixed-interest departments of investment firms. I remember meeting a fixed-interest manager working for a competitor at the time and it was almost as if I'd met someone from another profession – the jobs were so different. Also, we did our jobs with little knowledge of what was happening in other parts of the globe or how shares were valued there. The US, Far Eastern, European and UK desks were all relatively separate and didn't talk much to each other. As a UK specialist, I would have little knowledge about companies in similar businesses to my own holdings elsewhere in the world even in they competed against each other.

There were, of course, very few hedge funds in those days. Private equity existed but you rarely came across it if you were following equities – public to private deals were few and far between. Hedge funds have increased the competitive landscape with their often short-term focus and, with the growth of quant funds as well, more and more money is chasing short-term momentum. Trends therefore go on for longer and get more overdone (both up and down) than in the past. In some ways the market is more efficient, certainly in reacting to short-term events. However, I am convinced that the growth of hedge funds, momentum investors and quantitive funds all jumping on a trend has led to periods of mis-pricing and led to great opportunities for investors taking a longer-term view.

Another big change is in valuation models. In the early days we didn't get much further than PE and yield, maybe occasionally return on equity might be referred to. So the concept of companies needing to earn their cost of capital before they created value was a significant change. Many companies laboured for many years and investors happily put money in them, despite them not creating any value for shareholders. A result of this change is that there has been a permanent improvement in the return on capital of the average British listed company.

Companies are now far more responsive to shareholders. In the early days, surprisingly, many companies really didn't care about shareholders' views and concerns; particularly if their share price was of little interest to the management in the short term (sometimes, capital taxes actually meant some family-controlled companies wanted low shares prices). These were companies unwilling to meet shareholders or react to their views. I think the whole topic of shareholders becoming more involved in companies, voting shares, etc., has improved standards across the board. I believe the average British company today is far superior – both in terms of the way it runs the business and the job it does for shareholders. Therefore, on average, valuations deserve to be higher (particularly as today very few are not creating value for their shareholders). They are much more attractive investments than was the case in previous decades.

In many ways the City has changed for the better and it is a much more professional meritocracy, although maybe some of the fun has been lost along the way.

Some thoughts on the future of investment management

To finish this book I want to give my thoughts on five subjects of topical interest: stamp duty, private equity, hedge funds, activism and regulation.

Stamp duty has become a voluntary tax for many investors. Most hedge funds, many overseas investors and an increasing number of private investors avoid paying this tax by using mechanisms such as contracts for differences or betting on share price movements rather than buying actual shares. On the other hand, most domestic pension funds, insurance companies and unit and investment trusts do pay stamp duty. It seems to me unfair that traditional institutions that handle the bulk of the savings of the UK public are being penalised. Unless the rules change, I believe more and more institutions will start to use structures that avoid the tax and I can't blame them for doing so. This tax should either be abolished, getting rid of the double standard, or a level playing field should be created that doesn't disadvantage UK-based financial institutions.

Despite the cyclical downturn, private equity (PE) will remain a force in all financial markets. Over time, the funds raised by PE have become bigger and, as mentioned earlier in the book, as they become bigger the deals they do are likely to also become larger – but the larger the deal the fewer the avenues open to them to find suitable acquisition candidates. One area where there is the possibility of buying larger companies is on the stock market and I believe that these public-to-private deals will play a greater role once the current credit crisis has passed. Although this is good for investors who own shares in the companies bought out, I think it is less good in the long term. This is because it will lead to a shrinking of the universe that is available for investment, the possible removal of some sectors and the loss of specific companies that have unique investment characteristics. It is unlikely that there will be enough flotations of sufficient size to fill this gap.

What makes me even more concerned is the long-term brain drain from listed companies to PE – a lot of the best chief executives and finance directors are leaving the quoted sector for the potentially higher rewards. To limit this trend I believe two things need to happen. First, the average level of debt in UK listed companies needs to rise (the average level of debt to EBITDA is about 1.2 times and could comfortably be higher once normal credit conditions return without overleveraging companies). If this happened, there would be less opportunity for PE funds to buy these companies and gear them up substantially. Second, the rewards for executive directors of listed companies need to rise. I know this goes against the mood of many corporate governance policies but I am against trying to cap rewards for such directors (say by limits on absolute pay levels) – provided that the rewards are based on success and the definition of commercial success is fair. I believe in reward structures that align returns for shareholder and executive management.

Also, I have been a proponent of a type of listed stub equity in PE deals that allows investors who want to cash in on a bid to do so, particularly if they don't like the higher risks that higher gearing bring. It would also allow some shareholders to stay invested in the company after the bid goes through and therefore benefit from the potentially higher returns the new structure brings. I think this would be of particular interest to some institutional shareholders. To date such structures have only been used very rarely.

I have nothing against hedge funds and some of the best managers I've come across have ended up working for one. Their two plus twenty fee structure (2 per cent a year of assets plus 20 per cent of any gain) is a great draw but it entices into the industry some managers who aren't so good. In the past few years, hedge funds have changed from being the domain of wealthy individuals and family offices (traditionally, few were based in the UK) to being much more widely used by many mainstream institutional investors and there are now moves afoot to open them up to being bought by ordinary UK private investors. This change of client base has led to a huge influx of money into hedge funds. Nearly always in the investment business, when too much money flows into one area the returns from that area reduce. The influx of money has led a number of funds to be set up, sometimes with managers with unproved ability. Therefore, I believe that the returns from the average hedge fund are likely to fall and there will be more 'blow ups', particularly if levels of gearing available in the past are not available for the next couple of years and these newer investors are disappointed as a result. The credit crisis has led to fewer prime brokers, a reduction in their availability and an increase in the cost of the leverage that they will grant their hedge fund clients.

Running hedge funds with their investment freedom, ability to short as well as be long and their high fees is a magnet for many money managers and analysts. However, like so many things in investment it's not as easy as it looks and many new hedge funds fail (it is estimated that although 110 funds were launched in 2007, 550 closed). I recommend any aspiring hedge fund manager to read Barton Bigg's excellent description of the industry in *Hedgehogging* before they decide to change horses. If average returns are going to drop, as I think is likely, this will increase the fallout rate and a lot of funds will close in the next few years.

For a long time I wondered why companies were willing to do face-to-face meetings with hedge funds who were as likely to be short of their shares as be long of them. A couple of years ago, an obliging chief executive told me why: 'Most of the time we have better meetings with hedge fund managers than we do with the average long-only fund. If we are on a road show and having to do a large number of meetings we are keen that at least some of them are interesting meetings for us as management.' In general, they apparently found that the average hedge fund was better informed about their company and asked better questions. This was the basis for a much more interesting meeting than with many long-only funds who might just require the company to go through their presentation and asked few questions. He finished off by saying that the average Fidelity meeting was like a good hedge fund meeting because we did our homework and asked interesting questions (I don't think he was just being polite!). If he is correct, and I have no reason to doubt him, then many long-only funds are bringing on their own long-term demise if chief executives are less keen to meet them.

As hedge funds become more important to brokers, I have become increasingly concerned about the confidentiality of our own trading activity and views (nearly all our trading goes through brokers). Occasionally, brokers will try and get one of our analysts to say more than they should do about our views. Hedge funds pay a lot for a small information advantage and information leakage to brokers is a real risk.

One final observation on hedge funds is that the gap is closing between traditional long-only funds and hedge funds. Often today an investment management group will have both types of fund within the same organisation. Also, UCITS III, the European legislation that regulates undertakings for collective investment in transferable securities, has widened the activities that a traditional long-only fund manager is allowed to engage in. Two of the new activities are hedging and affectively being able to short stocks (so long-only is no longer long-only!). We received these powers on Fidelity Special Situations Fund in September 2006 after they were approved by a shareholders' vote. I think we will see more unit trusts and mutual funds take these powers. Given that the fee structure on a fund such as Fidelity Special Situations Fund is substantially below the average hedge fund I believe that such funds represent excellent value for money when run by a good fund manager at a reputable investment house.

My name has been closely associated with the activism trend and I remain a great proponent of considered activism. I think being an engaged shareholder is important and I believe that it is part of one's responsibility to be involved particularly if, like we do, you want a dialogue with companies and demand a lot of management time for meetings. Also, when my funds became large I was keen to find any activity that could give us an edge in managing large amounts of money. Activism has opened options for us where we are one of the larger shareholders in a company that is not doing well and where we believe if certain things changed, such as strategy or management, the company could perform better. I feel some UK shareholders have not been active enough as, say, with the managements of banks who must take part of the blame for the situation that many now find themselves in and the huge fall in share prices.

However, I am concerned about the trend of very short-term investors taking relatively small stakes in companies and trying to be very active. Already, the job of managements is difficult when they have different shareholders each with different views about the direction the company should go in. I have two worries: first, companies cannot be run successfully by taking very short-term decisions and if activists succeed in getting managements to do this they will change the corporate landscape in the UK for the worse; second, there seems to be a growing anti-activist movement that is even suggesting a curtailment of shareholder influence by removing voting rights in certain circumstances. This would also be a bad development in my view as it could weaken the influence bone fide institutions have over companies. We strongly support the one-share, one-vote principle. I am also against any legislation, as is being proposed in Germany, that stops professional investors being able to talk to each other about mutual investments. Nearly always before we engage with companies on a specific issue we will talk to other large investors in the particular company to see if they share our views.

I can't close this chapter without some reference to the current banking crisis and its long-term implications. Many commentators agree that one of the results will be regulation once the dust has settled. I only hope that, in their desire to tighten the rules, regulators do not throw the baby out with the bath water.

No doubt some of these regulations will affect the investment management business, but the main focus will be on the commercial and investment banks that are likely to find that leverage and capital ratios are more tightly controlled. For example, up until 2004 the leverage of the main US investment banks was constrained by legislation. These rules were relaxed and this is one of the reasons why the current crisis is as bad as it is. Such controls are likely to return. In addition, a more global framework to regulation is likely to emerge. In the global financial community that we are all part of, it is almost essential that regional or country regulators act together rather than in competition, or one after each other with a time lag. I think that much of the time UK regulators have been behind the curve, acting only after US or European regulators have acted. This has not been in the best interests of UK financial institutions and probably partially reflects the triumvirate nature of UK regulation (the Treasury, Bank of England and Financial Services Authority all being involved). I doubt whether our system will survive. Another area where national practices can conflict is where an investment bank such as Lehman goes bankrupt. The subsequent forms of administration varied from region to region, resulting in equity trades in some jurisdictions settling without problems but not doing so in others like the UK. If the UK keeps different administration procedures, London could lose out as institutions find it is safer to carry out trades in, say, Geneva than in London. In general, regulation should be a good thing and strengthen the financial system to help avoid crises like the current one where the banking system has come close to gridlock. As ever at such times, the scariest environments offer some of the best investment opportunities.

When I look back over the past 35 years or so, I count myself fortunate to have ended up, almost by chance, in an industry that has such attractive characteristics. It has seen phenomenal growth over this period. It's an activity where, I believe, the Anglo-Saxon world leads and London, at least during my investment career, has been one of the pre-eminent centres. It is an intellectually stimulating activity where I've had the opportunity to meet and question some of the best executives in the world. Additionally, I've been on top of nearly every business trend over this period, almost from the minute it started. Finally, it has brought me into contact with an interesting and talented group of people but, most important of all, it has been great fun. I've learnt a huge amount during that time and I hope I've been able to pass on some of this in these chapters.

Anthony Bolton's lessons from a life running money

Anthony Bolton's lessons from a life running money

Companies

- Start by evaluating the quality of the franchise
- Will it be here in ten years' time and be more valuable?
- Is the company in control of its own destiny?
- Is the business model easy to understand?
- Does the business generate cash?
- Remember, mean reversion is one of the great truisms of capitalism
- Beware company guidance
- Use part of a company meeting to talk about other companies
- If you have any doubts about a company, follow the cash

What to look for in management

- Integrity and openness are most important
- If you have any questions on competency or trustworthiness, avoid the company
- Do they have a detailed knowledge of the business strategically, operationally and financially?
- Are the objectives and incentives of management aligned with shareholders?
- Do the management's trades in the stock conflict or confirm their statements?
- Remember, people rarely change; invest in managers you trust

Shares

- Every stock you own should have an investment thesis

- Test this regularly and if no longer valid sell

- Look at a share the same way as if you were buying the whole business at that price

- Forget the price you paid for shares

- Keep an open mind and know the 'counter' thesis

- Think in terms of levels of conviction rather than price targets

- Don't try to make it back the way you lost it

- Consider six factors before you buy a share:

  - the quality of the business franchise;

  - the management;

  - the financials;

  - technical analysis of the share price history;

  - the valuation against history;

  - prospects for a takeover of the company

Sentiment

- Rate perception as important as reality

- Successful investment is a blend of standing your own ground while listening to the market

- Short term, the stock market is a voting machine, rather than a weighing machine

- Sentiment extremes, regardless of the underlying attraction of a share, can suggest major opportunity or risk

Constructing a portfolio

■ Position size should reflect conviction

■ Don't spend too much time on past performance attribution

■ Your portfolio should as nearly as possible reflect a 'start from scratch' portfolio

■ Don't pay too much attention to index weights

■ Make incremental rather than large moves

■ Never become emotionally attached to a holding

■ Investment is about making mistakes; win by not losing too often

■ Sell if the investment thesis is broken, if a stock reaches your valuation target or if you find something better

■ If in doubt about a holding or a possible new holding compare it directly against the most comparative stock that you own

■ Keep a balance between being on top of what you own and spending enough time looking for new ideas

Risks

■ My biggest mistakes have nearly always been companies with poor balance sheets

■ One loses the most money on highly geared companies when business conditions deteriorate

■ Remember that bad news doesn't travel well

■ Look at a share differently if it has performed well for several years; stocks with big unrealised profits in them are vulnerable in set backs

■ Avoid 'pass the parcel' stocks – overvalued stocks with

momentum – where investors hope there is more to go and they can sell them before the music stops

Financials

- Always read a company's announcements and information in the original – don't rely on a broker's summary
- Carefully read the notes that accompany accounts – key information can be hidden in the notes

Looking at valuations

- Don't look at one valuation measure, especially just a PE multiple
- Buying cheap shares gives you a margin of safety
- Valuation anomalies are more likely in medium-sized and small companies
- Look at today's valuation in the context of at least twenty-year historical valuations
- Buying when valuations are low against history substantially increases your chance of making money
- Never forget absolute valuations
- Remember that as a bull market progresses valuation methods typically get less conservative and vice versa

Takeovers and takeover targets

- Buy companies that have a M&A angle
- Big companies are less likely to be taken over

- The shareholder list can often carry clues about potential takeover candidates

- Be sceptical of being able to predict very short-term M&A targets

Favourite shares

- At the heart of my approach is buying cheaply valued recovery shares

- Favour unpopular shares

- Does a targeted company have a new management team with a clear and detailed recovery plan that you can track?

- You may have to buy a recovery stock before you have all the information

- Some of my best calls were in stocks that felt uncomfortable to buy

- Look for stocks with asymmetric pay-offs where you may make a lot of money but your downside is limited

- Value stocks outperform growth stocks in the long term

How to trade

- Delegate to a skilful trader and give them reasonable autonomy

- I only set tight limits on a minority of my trades

- Know when to be aggressive and know when to let the market come to you

- Avoid giving round number limits – this is what most other portfolio managers do

- Be patient – most stocks give you a second chance
- A block is normally the cheapest way to deal in size

Technical analysis

- The first thing I look at is the share chart
- Use technical analysis as a cross-check to your fundamental views
- Find an approach that works for you and then stick to it
- More useful for larger stocks
- Run profits and cut losses

Market timing

- Consistently successful market calls are very difficult to make
- If you're a private investor, take a long-term view. Don't put money in the stock market that you will need in the next three years
- Never underestimate the fact that the market is an excellent discounter of the future
- Don't be afraid to go against the general mode of the market
- Markets will react to expected positive or negative events in anticipation of those events
- Consider what is being assumed in share prices, rather than what the outlook is like
- In the mature stages of a bull market, prune back your holdings of more risky stocks
- Be most on your guard after a long upward move of four to five years

Bibliography

Biggs, B. (2006) *Hedghogging*, John Wiley

Brewster, D., *Memoirs of Newton*, vol. II, chapter 27

Buffett, M., and Clark, D. (2007) *The Tao of Warren Buffett*, Simon & Schuster

Buffett, W. (1983) Chairman's Letter, Berkshire Hathaway

Buffett, W. (1991) quoted in Grant, L. 'The $4-billion regular guy,' *Los Angeles Times*, 7 April, p36

Buffett, W. (1996) Chairman's Letter, Berkshire Hathaway

Buffett, W., and Jaffe, T. (1987) 'What we can learn from Phil Fisher,' *Forbes*, 19 October, p40

Churchill, W.S. (1949) *Great Contemporaries*, Odhams Press

Galbraith, J.K. (1961) *The Great Crash: 1929*, Pelican

Graham, B. (1949) *The Intelligent Investor*, Harper Collins

Graham, B. (1986) *Creating Shareholder Value: The new standard for business performance*, Collier Macmillan

Graham, B., and Dodd, D. (1934) *Security Analysis*, McGraw Hill

Grantham, G. (2006) GMO Special Topic Letter to the Investment Committee VIII, July

Kaufman, P.D. (2005) *Poor Charlie's Almanack: The wit and wisdom of Charles T. Munger*, Donning

Keynes, J.M. (1936) *General Theory of Employment, Interest and Money*, Harcourt, Brace

Kupfer, A., 'Gates on Buffett', *Fortune*, 5 February, p102

Legg Mason Shareholder's Letter (2005) fourth quarter (www.leggmason.co.uk)

Lynch, P., and Rothchild, J. (1993) *Beating the Street*, Simon & Schuster

Miller, B. (2005) 'Investor Insight – Bill Miller,' in *Value Investor Insight*, 2005

Miller, B. (2008) Legg Mason Investment Letter, 2 October (www.leggmason.co.uk)

Rappaport, A. (2000) *Creating Shareholder Value: A guide for managers and investors*, Simon & Schuster

Summers, L.H. (2003) speech as president of Harvard University

Taleb, N.N. (2005) *Fooled by Randomness*, Random House

Templeton, J. (1995) quoted in Minard, L. 'The principle of maximum pessimism,' *Forbes*, 16 January, p67

Train, J. (1994) 'The Icarus syndrome: in the pink,' *Financial Times*, Weekend Money, 26 November, p2

Zeikel, A. (1983) 'Organizing for creativity,' *Financial Analysts Journal*, Nov–Dec, pp25–29